"In *Single Ever After*, Dani Treweek offers a hopeful, helpful guide through a topic still viewed with much suspicion or sadness, or both. She leads her readers through rich biblical, theological, and personal territory to point to God's positive vision for the single life: a vision that is an encouragement to both single and married disciples. The New Testament loves to call Christians 'brothers and sisters in Christ', and this book helps us grow into that reality, which is so much more than mere metaphor."

RACHEL GILSON, Author, *Born Again This Way: Coming Out, Coming to Faith, and What Comes Next*

"This hit the spot: fresh turns of phrase, deep theological reflection and lots of pastoral wisdom. How can anyone do all three at once? Whether thinking about individual biblical texts or awkward scenarios over coffee after church, Dani Treweek guides us in our concerns about singleness, sex and marriage delicately and deliberately towards our heavenly home. May our churches be beacons of relational hope in an anxious world!"

RHYS BEZZANT, Principal, Ridley College, Australia; Visiting Fellow, Yale Divinity School

"Too many single women and men have been harmed by badly understood and applied Bible teaching on singleness, marriage and sex. Dani does us all a massive favour by returning to the key texts and understanding and applying them in life-giving ways. The positive vision of singleness that results needs to be heard not just by single Christians but by their pastors and friends. All of this comes well wrapped in eye-opening personal stories, Dani's good sense of humour, and her years of listening well to God and his people. This book is a much-needed gift to our churches today."

ED SHAW, Pastor, Emmanuel City Centre, Bristol, UK; r.livingout.org; ntimacy Deficit

T0407913

"As a 'never-married, older single person', I have read my fair share of books on singleness. For me, this one is the best of the bunch! It has a depth of theology, alongside a warmth and humour, which wonderfully engages the heart and the mind. Reading Dani's book felt like sitting down with a wise friend and listening as she reminds us of God's goodness and grace in whatever context he places us. Whether you're single or married, this one's a winner!"

JENNY SALT, Associate to Archdeacon of Women's Ministry, Sydney Anglican Diocese; Podcast host, *Salt—Conversations with Jenny*

"Provocative and pastoral, *Single Ever After* offers a fresh way of thinking about singleness: not as a death sentence but as a signpost to the resurrection life that followers of Jesus will enjoy with him forever! Whether you are single or married, I highly recommend you grab a copy of this book. It's urgent that we start to think better and more biblically about both singleness and marriage, and *Single Ever After* could be just the shot in the arm we need!"

REBECCA MCLAUGHLIN, Author, *Confronting Christianity: 12 Hard Questions for the World's Largest Religion*

"*Single Ever After* gives a gloriously good vision for singleness here and now by pointing to how it foreshadows how all Christians will live for eternity. While being realistic about the challenges and sorrows of singleness, Dani shows how it is intrinsically good. Her exposition of 1 Corinthians was clear and profoundly encouraging, which is not often how this passage feels to singles. *Single Ever After* is essential reading for church leaders as they consider how to care for those in their church who are single and single-again."

RACHEL SLOAN, Director for Women's Ministry, Fellowship of Independent Evangelical Churches (FIEC), UK

Single Ever After

Danielle Treweek

thegoodbook
COMPANY

For all my single brothers and sisters who it has been a privilege to know in this life...

And for all those I'm looking forward to getting to know in the ever after to come.

Single Ever After
© Danielle Treweek, 2025

Published by:
The Good Book Company

thegoodbook.com | thegoodbook.co.uk
thegoodbook.com.au | thegoodbook.co.nz

Cover design by Drew McCall

ISBN: 9781802543261 | JOB-008254 | Printed in India

Contents

I Still Haven't Found What I'm Looking For

If, 25 years ago, you had told me that there'd come a day when I'd have a PhD in singleness, two books on the topic and a ministry devoted to it... *and* that I'd still be single myself, I'd have politely insisted that you clearly had the wrong Dani. And then I'd probably have run from the room.

Like most Christian teens and young adults, I grew up expecting to get married. Becoming a wife and a mother seemed wonderfully inevitable—the natural and expected path for my life. And yet, as I now settle into what I prefer to think of as "prime time" rather than middle age, that path hasn't materialised. Instead, here I am: a Doctor of Singleness.

While so many of my friends seemed to move seamlessly through first meetings, awkward conversations, dating, engagements, weddings, honeymoons and baby announcements, it just never happened for me. Despite my best hopes, prayers and efforts, single I remained.

I didn't quite know what to do with that. And honestly, it seemed that nobody else did either. As my twenties turned into my thirties, I tried to make sense of being single in a church culture that seemed to idealise—at times even idolise—marriage and family. But the sermons, books, podcasts, conferences and conversations all seemed to point to the same conclusion: there simply was little purpose to Christian singleness. At best, it could be put to good use in filling up the church rosters. At worst, it was treated as an unmitigated tragedy.

My dissatisfaction with this state of affairs became even more pronounced once I began to serve in vocational women's ministry. Never-married women, divorced women, widows and single mothers—there were far more of them in the pews than I had ever realised. These women (along with their male counterparts, who were fewer in number but nonetheless very much present) were grappling with the same longing for belonging in their singleness that I was. They would come to me, hoping I had the answers. I didn't.

And yet, when I opened the Bible, I could see that it had plenty to say on the subject.

Passages like 1 Corinthians 7 celebrate singleness. Our Saviour lived and loved on earth as a single man. The apostle responsible for authoring about half of the New Testament was unmarried. While Scripture beautifully honours marriage, it devotes even greater attention to the relationships between brothers and sisters in the household of God. And the thing that most captured my spiritual imagination was Jesus' promise that in the resurrection age *none* of us would be married to one another. According to him, we will all be "single" ever after (Matthew 22:29-30).

I could see that God's word didn't just speak to the topic of singleness—it spoke to me in *my* singleness. I was confident that there *were* God-given answers to be had about my purpose and place of belonging as an unmarried Christian. And so, I went searching for those answers.

This book is (part of) the fruit of that search.

Each chapter explores a particular conception—or, more often, misconception—about singleness in the Christian life and community. We'll examine *what* Christians today tend to think about singleness, marriage, sex, friendship, church and more; *why* we think what we think; and *how* the Bible compels us to reshape or reorient aspects of our thinking.

But this isn't just a book about thinking. It's also a book about living. And so, the "Living It Out" discussion that follows each chapter is designed to help translate biblical truths into relational action (meaning that the two parts are best read together). In each of those, we'll consider how a truly biblical view of singleness might nurture and transform our relationships with Jesus and with others.

All of which means that this book is for both the 20-year-old single Christian excited about the prospect of marriage and also the 40-year-old who wonders if it will ever happen. It's for the 32-year-old divorced single father and the 69-year-old widowed grandmother. It's for those eagerly anticipating marriage and those grieving its absence; it's for those single by choice and those single by circumstance; it's for the content, the discontent, and those who feel both— sometimes, like me, at the very same time.

But this book isn't just for singles. It's also for their married friends and their church pastors. If that's you, I'm so glad you're reading these words. We, your single brothers and sisters, need your support as we seek to live for Jesus. We need your help to live out our singleness within our church family faithfully. We need you to love us well in our singleness and to help us love you well in it, too.

All of that requires you to not only understand singleness itself but to understand *us in our singleness.*

Finally, this is a book about singleness but for everyone because, while only some of us will remain single—or become single again—in this life, in the eternal life to come, all of God's people will be *Single Ever After*.

Waiting On the World to Change

Part 1: Specialising in Eternity

A few years ago, I came across a terrarium for purchase online. It was a glass jar, about the size and shape of a fishbowl. Inside it lay a gorgeous miniature landscape of a live-moss-covered cliff covered in a few scattered plastic palm trees. Blue resin waves broke over synthetic rocks at the cliff's base. Okay, yes, it was almost entirely artificial. But as soon as the algorithms brought it up on my social-media feed, well, I couldn't look away. And gee whiz, what do you know? I just so happened to have a birthday in a few weeks' time.

And so, I oh-so-casually showed it to my family. My sister was sceptical and with good reason. She knew my poor track record at keeping any kind of green thing alive. My mother was a little confused by my new-found preoccupation with terrariums. Nonetheless, I could tell that she was dutifully picking up on the hints that I was not so subtly laying down. But for his part, my ever practically minded father looked at the picture for a bit before turning to me with a quizzical frown and asking, "Okay, but, well, what does it actually *do*?"

What Does Singleness Actually Do?

If you are an unmarried Christian, I imagine there has been a time (perhaps many times) when you've looked at your singleness and thought to yourself, "Okay, but, well, what does it actually do? What is it good for?" Perhaps you have even wondered, "What am I good for?" We've been taught that God has his purposes in every area of our lives—but it's hard to figure out what they are in this.

If you've found yourself confronted by these kinds of questions, you're not alone. As a never-married woman, I've often wondered what the point of my singleness is. And I know many other single men and women—never-married, divorced and widowed—who wrestle with the same questions and anxieties.

Why am I single (or single again)?

Why am I the only one of my friends who somehow ended up without a spouse, kids, a family to call my own?

What are other people thinking about my singleness? Do they pity me? Regard me with suspicion? Think that it's a shame?

Why do I feel so alone in trying to understand the purpose of my situation? *Is* there even a purpose?

Those are some of the questions that this chapter—and this book—will seek to answer.

But first, we need to consider some of the ways in which we're prone to get this wrong. For example, a few years ago, the Christian multimedia platform *Relevant* published an online article called "Singleness Is Not a Problem That Needs to Be Fixed". The article begins with these words:

If you're a Christian, older than 22 and single, odds are things are weird for you sometimes. Intentionally or not, the Church seems to have expectations, and even a timeline, for when people who are single will grow up and get married. If we operate outside of that trajectory, we are often treated as if we have some sort of problem. You'd think there was some hidden Scripture that says, "Thou shall be marriedeth by this time, or thou be a freak."[1]

The author goes on to say that singleness "can be a gift from God. That's right … Not a curse. Not a source of pity. Not a problem".

But, what exactly is it about singleness that leads him to see it as a gift rather than a problem? Well, he suggests that single people not only avoid the "challenges" of marriage, but they also have more energy and time for ministry. In other words, the purpose of singleness is having more time to do more of the good things you have more energy to do… all because you aren't dealing with the hard stuff of marriage.

This is what I call an "instrumental" understanding of singleness. Not "instrument" like a guitar or a piano but instead like a fork or a shovel. That is, singleness is seen as a tool that has a specific utility. It is something that helps you *do* a particular thing.

While this instrumental approach to singleness is on view in that *Relevant* article, it is certainly not unique to it. In fact, this has been the dominant understanding of singleness throughout the Protestant church of the West for centuries. We tend not to think that singleness has meaning in and of itself, but just that it can be meaningfully spent. Which also means that when we see someone who does not seem to be using their singleness "properly", well, we think that they aren't "doing singleness" right—that they are missing the point of their being unmarried.

To borrow (and somewhat adapt) the words of that *Relevant* article, *You'd think there was some hidden Scripture that says, "Thou shall be marriedeth by this time, or spending thy singleness in ways others deemeth good. Otherwise, thou art a selfish sinner who is putting off their cleareth duty to marry post-haste."*

Intrinsic Versus Instrumental

Now, you might be thinking, "Well, surely singleness is good because it gives you more time and energy and focus to serve God!" And, yes, singleness is good because of all the gospel-oriented ways in which we can serve through it. Yet, singleness is not only *instrumentally* good. It is also *intrinsically* good. And we only need to look to marriage to understand the difference.

Christians have long held that God designed marriage to fulfil some very important purposes or "goods". Procreation is a good of marriage. Intimacy and faithful companionship is another. Marriage's role as a relational anchor within our broader social order is yet another still. People throughout church history have used different words to describe these goods, and the lines between them can be a little blurry at times, but the point is this: Christians have always believed that the goods of marriage mean that each marital relationship is *instrumentally* significant. To put it plainly, we see marriage as being useful for individuals, households, communities and societies as a whole.

But our understanding of marriage doesn't stop there, because we don't only believe marriage *provides* important goods but that it also *is* an important good. We believe marriage is a good in and of itself. The Bible teaches that the ultimate purpose of marriage is not found in what we do with our individual marital unions but in what that one-flesh union itself is purposed for:

> *"For this reason a man will leave his father and mother and be united to his wife, and the two will become one flesh." This is a profound mystery—but I am talking about Christ and the church.*
>
> *(Ephesians 5:31-32, quoting Genesis 2:24)*

As Paul wrote to the Ephesian Christians about the relationship between a husband and wife, he referred them back to the very first teaching on marriage—indeed the very first instance of marriage—in Scripture. But then Paul does something rather unexpected. He says that the profound mystery that Genesis 2:24 is really talking about is not ultimately about human husbands and wives at all! Instead, marriage is and has always been about Christ and the church.

Right back at the very beginning, God designed human marriage to have a purpose. It was to act as a preview, a signpost, a foreshadowing of the better, greater, more wonderful and more enduring union to come—the marriage between Christ and the church. Paul takes his readers back to creation to explain that truth. But the author of Revelation takes us forward to the new creation to make precisely the same point. In his vision of that new creation, John hears a great multitude shouting:

> *Hallelujah!*
> *For our Lord God Almighty reigns.*
> *Let us rejoice and be glad*
> *and give him glory!*
> *For the wedding of the Lamb has come,*
> *and his bride has made herself ready.*

Fine linen, bright and clean,
was given her to wear. (Revelation 19:6-8)

A little later, John describes seeing the new Jerusalem, "coming down out of heaven from God, prepared as a bride beautifully dressed for her husband" (Revelation 21:2). Who is the bride—this new Jerusalem? It is the church, the people of God. And who is the husband waiting at the end of the heavenly aisle? It is Jesus Christ, the Lamb of God.

This, if we stop to think about it, may all sound a little weird. But that's only because we've not yet come to experience the full reality of it. And this is exactly why earthly marriage is so important. The relationship between a husband and wife is meant to provide us with a glimpse of the uniquely exclusive, deeply intimate and lovingly faithful union that God's people—together as the church—will one day enjoy with our Saviour. Marriage points beyond itself to foreshadow something greater than itself: the ultimate marriage to come.

And so human marriage doesn't just *do* good things here and now, like enabling child-bearing and strengthening the social order. No, it *is* itself a good thing because it is designed to point to something beyond itself. It has what we might call an *intrinsic* meaning and purpose that go beyond the here and now. Marriage's ultimate meaning is found in its eternal end.

However, we don't tend to think the same way about singleness. We're happy to say that singleness can achieve good things here and now. But we don't usually see singleness as having a meaning or significance beyond that—as having its own eternal end.

This can leave those of us who are single feeling that our life situation is only a good thing if we are constantly making sure we do all the right stuff with it. And so, having a purely instrumental view of singleness can rob us of any joy or dignity in simply being unmarried. It can also mean that other Christians deem our singleness not to be a good thing if, in their eyes, we're not doing enough of all that good stuff with it. That is, they may think there isn't any joy or dignity in simply being unmarried.

On that count, Jesus Christ himself shows us that we are wrong.

We're All Gonna Be "Single" For Ever

The Gospel author Matthew records an encounter between Jesus and a group of Jewish religious leaders called the Sadducees. As a child, I was taught the Sadducees were "sad, you see" because they didn't believe in life after death—a cringeworthy but undeniably memorable pun! This meant that they were a little perturbed by this Jesus fellow going around teaching Jews about a future day of resurrection for all God's people. So, they come up with a clever plan to entrap him by using the hypothetical story of a very unfortunate woman:

> "Teacher," they said, "Moses told us that if a man dies without having children, his brother must marry the widow and raise up offspring for him. Now there were seven brothers among us. The first one married and died, and since he had no children, he left his wife to his brother. The same thing happened to the second and third brother, right on down to the seventh. Finally, the woman died. Now then, at the resurrection, whose wife will she be of the seven, since all of them were married to her?"
>
> (Matthew 22:24-28)

The story is a kind of overblown riddle intended to back Jesus into an intellectual corner. You can almost imagine the Sadducees standing before him with raised eyebrows and smug smirks: *So, Jesus, if this life after death you are going on about is real, try and get yourself out of this!* But of course, Jesus is unfazed. He replies:

> *You are in error because you do not know the Scriptures or the power of God. At the resurrection people will neither marry nor be given in marriage; they will be like the angels in heaven. (v 29-30)*

The Sadducees had made a foolish mistake. They had assumed that the resurrection age Jesus was preaching about would be exactly like this age—at least with respect to marriage. Jesus tells them that this is a false assumption. At the resurrection, this hypothetical woman would not be married to *any* of those men. Why? Because resurrected people will neither marry nor be given in marriage.

Jesus couldn't have simply meant there wouldn't be any new marriages in the resurrection age. If that was the case, the Sadducees' question about which of the men she'd call her husband would still stand. No, in the resurrection age, there will be *no* marriage of any kind between men and women. Instead, we will be like the angels—that is, we will not marry, we will not have sex and we will not procreate. The new creation will not be filled with many wives and husbands. Instead there will be one husband (Jesus) and one wife (the church).

So, if we will not be husbands and wives to each other, what *will* we be? Well, the New Testament shows us that the primary relationship Jesus' people will share then is the same one we share now—we will be each other's brothers and sisters in Christ. In fact, the New Testament describes us now as each other's siblings over 180 times— including in John's vision of heaven in Revelation (6:11). This familial connection is not temporary or for this earth only. According to Scripture, "those who believed in [Jesus'] name" have been given "the right to become children of God" (John 1:12-13). Those who have been made God's children for eternity have also been made each other's siblings for eternity. And so, in the time that comes after time, the enduring relationships of resurrected men and women won't be those of husbands and wives but of brothers and sisters in Christ.

You, I, all of us... we are gonna be *single* siblings. Forever. This means that it is not just marriage that acts as a signpost towards eternity. Because of who we now are in Jesus, singleness also points us towards a *different aspect* of the future reality that awaits us. Those of us who are not married *now* are living, breathing, walking, talking examples of the relational life that awaits us all in the new creation.

Now, of course, there is a sense in which *all* Christians are already living the relational life awaiting us in the age to come. We are all already brothers and sisters to each other. But those of us who are unmarried have a kind of leg-up in that department. Unlike our married counterparts, we already experience the kind of relational life that doesn't include one unique and exclusive relationship with one other person. We already relate to *all* other Christians as simply brother or sister. Our relational lives here and now most closely resemble the relational life among God's people to come there and then.

Certainly, we are not yet perfected examples of that coming reality. For that, we all need to wait for Jesus to return. And yet, as those with no exclusive, one-flesh relationship with another person in this life, our lives provide unique glimpses of the relational life we'll share with all other sons and daughters of God on the other side of resurrection day.

All of this means that married and single Christians *both* specialise in depicting eternity.

Specialising in Eternity... Together

Just as one medical doctor's speciality might be in dermatology while another's is in cardiology, married and single Christians have a different speciality focus. The married Christian specialises in pointing us towards the gloriously intimate relationship which the church (that is, all of us together) will enjoy with Christ for ever. The unmarried Christian specialises in pointing us towards the gloriously intimate relationships we will enjoy with one another within the church for ever. We are complementary— rather than competing—co-specialists in eternity.

We so often get this wrong. For some reason, we tend to think of marriage and singleness as opponents. We think that to speak honourably about one means we must diminish the honour of the other. We think that to say one is good means we must automatically mean the other is less good.

But the glorious future awaiting us is one in which marriage and singleness will perfectly co-exist. The church will delight in her marriage to Christ, and we, as individual members of the church, will delight in our unmarried relationships with one another. Both situations are instrumentally good in this life. And both situations are intrinsically good because of the life to come.

So Jesus' people who are married and Jesus' people who are single are not opponents or adversaries. Rather, they are brothers and sisters who need one another to help keep their eyes fixed on the full glory of the resurrection life ahead. Married and single Christians are both God's co-specialists in depicting eternity.

Waiting On the World to Change

Part 2: Living It Out

As resurrected people, in our relationships with each other, we're all gonna be "single" ever after.

Whether we are married or single, that idea can be a difficult one to contemplate. How can we have confidence that eternity will be so amazing (let alone perfect!) if it doesn't include something we think of as so very good, and even necessary, for human flourishing?

Well, we can—and should—have confidence because we believe in a truthful and trustworthy God. He has promised that even the best of what this life has to offer won't be able to compare with what will be eternally ours in Christ. We may not be able to get our heads around what eternal life as *single* resurrected men and women will be like. But that's to be expected—we are not there yet! But we are, nonetheless, called to trust in God's promises about that future. Indeed, we are called to set our hearts and minds on them:

Since, then, you have been raised with Christ, set your hearts on things above, where Christ is, seated at the

right hand of God. Set your minds on things above, not
on earthly things. (Colossians 3:1-2)

The things above are not given as far-off ideas for us to
contemplate casually. No, they are what we are to set our
hearts and minds on *here and now*. And so, the knowledge
that we will one day be resurrected people who are
together married to Christ but individually *single* for ever
has relevance now. It matters.

We'll see that putting this biblical truth into practice will
have different implications for those of us who are single
and those of us who are not. But first, there is one very
important, even primary, lesson that *all* of the body of
Christ are called to put into practice together.

We Are Family

We have seen that the relationship between a husband
and wife is *not* the primary, enduring, eternal, ultimate
relationship that will exist between resurrected Christian
people. Before (and after) we are someone's spouse, we
are their sibling in Christ. This is who the church is. We
are the household of God. We are sons and daughters of
the same heavenly Father. We are brothers and sisters
through the blood of his Son.

This means that when we meet together—when
we pray for each other, worship in song together, sit
under God's word alongside one another and carry each
others' burdens—we do so not as members of many
different households; we do so as members of one
household. The church is not an affiliation of individual
families who happen to meet together in the same place
at the same time. No, the church is *one new family*. And
in that family, married and single people equally belong
to each other.

I grew up attending an Anglican church. In the middle of an Anglican service—right after we have prayed in confession together and have been reminded of the forgiveness we all have in Christ—everything suddenly stops. We all get up from our seats, wander around to stand beside others, look them directly in the eye and, with a shake of their hand or even a hug, say, "Peace be with you". It must feel a bit bizarre to newcomers! But what is happening in that moment is a truly beautiful thing. It is a living demonstration of how our peace with God means we have peace with each other. In that moment, the old turn to the young, the men to the women, the rich to the poor, the healthy to the sick, the lifelong Christians to the brand new Christians, the married to the single, and we recognise that other person as our precious brother or sister.

Not so long ago, a married friend of mine named Katherine expressed her frustration about this moment in her own church. She said that so many of the married people in her church turn to their spouse, kiss them tenderly on their cheek, say, "Peace be with you", and then turn back to face the front. Even those who *do* "pass the peace" to someone else usually give them a cursory handshake before quickly turning away. "They are missing the whole point!" Katherine exclaimed in exasperation. And she is right. As church members, we stand alongside each other as relational equals. Christians who are husbands are first and foremost their wife's brother in Christ. Wives are first and foremost their husband's sister in Christ. And both husband and wife share that exact same glorious sibling relationship with all those they are not married to.

As we've seen, this wonderful truth is witnessed to by the intrinsic purpose of *both* marriage and singleness. Marriage reminds us of the glorious unity we share as the church, the bride of Christ. Singleness reminds us of the wonderful multiplicity of sibling relationships we share as individual members of the church. This is one way in which both marriage and singleness co-specialise in previewing eternity. But there are also others.

Single Specialists

If you are single, God intends your relationships within the church—yes, *your* humble, flawed, complicated, imperfect yet intrinsically wonderful relationships as an unmarried Christian—to be a signpost to the life to come. The fact that you don't have an exclusive covenanted relationship with one other person points towards the new creation in which none of us will have that relationship with any others.

And so, your singleness is vitally important. It's not meant to be insular or inward-looking. It's not meant to be tucked away, treated by you or others as a pity or a shame or a tragedy. It's not meant to be closed off, locked down, or written off as a missed opportunity. No, the rest of the church needs your singleness! We need you to live out the profound truth that marriage, romance and sex may be good, but they are not essential to what it means to be human. We need you to remind us of what we're all eagerly longing for—an eternity of deep, rich, valuable, intimate relationships shared between brothers and sisters in Christ. So, please, live your singleness out visibly within the body of Christ.

But what does this mean in practice? Well, it means consistently showing how important it is to cultivate an abundance of sibling relationships within the household of God. It means proactively opening your life up to a wide range of brothers and sisters. It means intentionally investing in and serving others.

It is both my own personal and my observed experience that we single Christians (especially those who have remained unmarried beyond young adulthood) often find it difficult to open ourselves up to others: to put ourselves out there relationally, to let others—and especially our married friends—know how we long to love and be loved. Perhaps that comes from low self-esteem or because we want to protect ourselves from rejection. Perhaps we are just too used to going it alone. Whatever the cause, we singles often feel that we need to take up as little space as possible in the lives of others. It's as though we need to make sure we are not a burden or inconvenience to them.

Yet, if we are family to each other—and we are!—then we need to push back on any feelings of insecurity and reluctance. We are siblings in Christ, who are called to love one another and carry each other's burdens.

But if others are to love us, then they need to know us. And if others are to help carry our burdens, then they need to know what those burdens are. And so we singles need to allow others to love us by allowing them to get to know us.

This will take courage and boldness. Getting to know people can be difficult (especially the older we get). Continuing to invest in and strengthen those relationships takes ongoing effort. And because of the busyness and chaos of family life, the responsibility for initiating that effort often seems to fall on the single person.

This is something I've had to grapple with over the years. I am good friends with numerous Christian couples, all of whom lead busy lives, with homes full of children of various ages and stages. I know these friends love hanging out with me as much as I love hanging out with them. But if I don't get in touch to organise a time to catch up, often it just won't happen.

For a long time, I quietly resented how I didn't seem to be on their relational radar as much as they were on mine. Eventually, though, I came to realise that their inability to initiate wasn't an indication of how they felt about me. It was simply a result of the sheer busyness of their lives (and their minds!). When I removed the chip from my shoulder, I realised that they were *thankful* when I reached out to them. They were always eager to see me. Now I welcome the responsibility of initiating because I recognise that it is a way I can love them in their needs while also providing them with the opportunity to love me in mine.

This is just one example of how those of us who are single can be proactive and intentional in pointing forward to eternity. Though, perhaps you may be thinking, "Aren't we back to the instrumentality of singleness after all? That idea that my singleness is only worthwhile and meaningful if I do this particular thing with it?"

Well, not quite. You see, there is a difference between saying singleness is only meaningful and good if used to do the right things and saying that singleness has intrinsic meaning that we are called to do something truly good with. In the first, the dignity of singleness is entirely dependent on what we do (or don't do) with it. But in the second, God has given singleness its own distinct dignity, and this is something which the gospel compels us to live out loudly.

That subtle shift in perspective changes everything. It frees us up as single Christians to embrace the goodness of our singleness even when our singleness may not feel good to us. To delight in the significance of our singleness even as we may be praying that God would lead us into marriage. To help others to see that our singleness has value even as we may be struggling with contentment in it.

As we'll see throughout the rest of this book, the single Christian life of this age is not always easy or comfortable. It can be difficult to open yourself up to that myriad of relationships. It can be exhausting to feel that the responsibility for initiating so often falls back on you. It can be painful to long for the goodness of marriage while never having that longing fulfilled. It can hurt to see friendships change, even diminish, when the arrival of a friend's new spouse suddenly interrupts long-established relational rhythms.

And yet, whatever your experience of it, your singleness itself remains good, dignified and meaningful because it reminds you—and the rest of us—of the time to come when our relationships with each other *won't* be difficult or exhausting or painful. It helps us set our eyes on the day when we will all stand shoulder to shoulder and with one voice sing praises to the one who has made us his children (Revelation 7:9-10). If you are a single Christian, then you are a specialist in depicting *that* eternity!

Married Specialists

If you are married, then you are also a specialist in depicting eternity. God intends your relationship with your spouse—yes, *your* humble, flawed, complicated, imperfect yet intrinsically wonderful relationship—to be a signpost to the life to come. Your one-flesh union foreshadows the bigger, better and more enduring union between Christ and his bride.

And so your marriage is vitally important. Yes, to you and your spouse. But to the rest of us as well. Your brothers and sisters in Christ, extended family, neighbours and colleagues need your marriage. They need you to live out that profound mystery *among them*.

But what does that actually look like? Well, to be honest, at this point I found myself scratching my head a little. So I reached out to some married friends and asked for some specific examples of how they intentionally try to live out the profound mystery of their marriage in a way that points to eternity.

However, as their responses began to roll in, I felt that they might not have really understood what I was asking—because they were just telling me stuff about how they try to be a good husband or wife. Anthony told me that it's about "advocating for each other and assuming the best of each other". Julie said that it lies in "our commitment to our marriage and forgiveness of each other despite our imperfections". Edwina shared that her husband "loves my body as his own. He notices when I'm not sleeping well or if I'm wound up". Josh said that he and his wife "try and disagree well, especially in front of our kids, so that we all see confession, forgiveness and reconciliation in action".

I read all of this thinking, "Well, that's all very nice, but... it wasn't exactly what I was wanting from them". I was hoping for some specific examples of how my friends use their marriages to take the focus off their own relationship so that they can put it on the coming marriage between Jesus and the church. But then, as I read back over their responses, I realised that it was actually I who had missed the whole point.

My friends' responses taught me that married Christians don't specialise in previewing eternity by taking the focus off of their relationship but *by putting the focus very much on it!* They foreshadow the life to come by fulfilling their promises to each other in the here and now. Promises to be each other's advocates, to forgive each other, to love each other's bodies, to pursue reconciliation and more—all these point to the passionate, committed, never-failing, reconciling love that Jesus has for his people.

If you are married, then this is *your* eternal specialty. However—and this is fundamental—for your marriage to be the signpost it is intended to be, you are not only called to love your husband or wife faithfully, sacrificially, servant-heartedly, consistently and extravagantly... but also *publicly*. To put it another way, if your marriage is going to be a signpost to eternity for anyone other than just the two of you, then we need to be able to see your marriage in action. And so, please, don't keep your relationship absolutely private. Don't keep your marriage firmly tucked away behind your household door. Instead, let us see you love each other (especially in all the messiness) because, as you do, you'll allow the rest of us to catch glimpses of eternity and so long for it all the more.

All by Myself

Part 1: The Not-Goodness of Adam's Aloneness

Given that I am by no means an outdoorsy person, my obsession with History Channel's *Alone* came as an unexpected development. And yet I've spent the last few years binge watching every season I could find.

For those unfamiliar with the show, ten contestants are separately deposited in extremely rugged and remote terrain. They take with them ten survival items and double their weight in camera equipment, all the better to film themselves going a little bit insane or starving to death—or both. While their goal is to be the last man or woman standing, they can pick up their satellite phone and "tap out" at any point that things become too much. The psychological drama is ramped up by the fact that none of them know how many other contestants remain in the game.

For me, the most fascinating thing about *Alone* is that it's not usually the threat of being eaten by a bear, freezing to death in the Arctic or licking tree bark for all their nutritional needs that causes many contestants to pick up that satellite phone. So many of them "tap out" for one profoundly simple reason: they can't bear the soul-crushing reality of being truly alone for another moment.

If there is any human person alive today who most resembles Adam's reality in the Garden of Eden, I reckon it would be one of those *Alone* contestants. In Genesis 2:18 we get this stark assessment of Adam's existence in a single-occupancy paradise:

> The LORD God said, "It is not good for the man to be alone. I will make a helper suitable for him."
>
> (Genesis 2:18)

Millennia later, many of us are tempted to make a similar assessment on life as a single person: *Not good.*

Being Alone and Being Lonely

In 2023, the Christian organisation Communio published a report titled "Nationwide Study on Faith and Relationships".[2] The report notes that while Sunday churchgoers report a significantly lower rate of loneliness than the average American, there is nonetheless "a substantial gap between married, cohabiting, and single Sunday churchgoers in feelings of loneliness".[3] It concludes that unmarried American churchgoers are three and one-third times more likely to experience or report being lonely than their married counterparts.[4]

If you are an unmarried Christian, then these statistics probably won't come as a surprise to you. Sadly, many singles find church to be a very lonely place. Liz told me she is at her loneliest when she arrives at church and "there's no one to sit with. I'm always on my own. It's exhausting, and I often arrive late to avoid this feeling." Steven says that when he was married, he and his family were regularly included in the plans of other people at his church. Now that he is a single father, this has become rare. One of the most heartbreaking stories I've heard came from my never-married friend Kelly. I'll let her tell it in her own words:

One Sunday morning at church, there were two occasions when the worship leader invited everyone to pray with their neighbours during the service. Mindful of the awkwardness people can feel when praying out loud or with strangers, I glanced to my left to engage the people next to me; but the man quickly turned his head and began praying with his wife. In front of me, the same thing happened. As I disappointedly stared at the families across the room, my cheeks grew hot with tears. Some time later I shared my experience with a woman who hadn't married until her late 30s. She responded, "Well, I don't think I would have been comfortable with my husband inviting you to pray with us either". I once again concluded that church really is one of the loneliest places for a single person.

The statistics and stories above reflect the painful lived experience of many single Christians. And so the question we are left with is this: How can we resolve the large disparity between the relational experiences of single and married Christians in the church today? How do we make sure nobody feels lonely within their church family?

Communio's "Nationwide Study on Faith and Relationships" report proposes an answer to this question. It suggests that the "loneliness data for those who have never married reinforces the truth found in Genesis 2:18, that 'It is not good for man to be alone'".[5] That is, the report holds that single people are *destined* to feel lonely in church simply because they are not married. In the words of the report itself, the "data on the loneliness gap between single and married churchgoers reinforces the ongoing importance of marriage as a major solution for what ails the Church and her people".[6]

But is loneliness within the community of God's people truly an inevitable part of the experience of someone who does not have a husband or a wife? Are those of us who are single (or single again) doomed to find ourselves for ever on the margins of our church family? To answer those questions, we need to explore what is—and what is not— going on in Genesis 2:18.

What Was Not Good?

In the beginning, there was absolutely nothing. And then God spoke, and nothing became everything. In Genesis 1, we read that God looked at each thing he spoke into existence and he saw it was good. And yet, it was not until God made humanity in his own image that what was good turned into something "very good" (v 31).

If Genesis 1 gives us the bird's-eye view of God's act of creation, then Genesis 2 is like a camera lens that zooms in on a particular part of the action. We discover how God created the man and placed him in the glorious garden. Adam was living his best life! But then suddenly, in the midst of all this abundant goodness, there is something not good: "The LORD God said, 'It is not good for the man to be alone. I will make a helper suitable for him'" (v 18). Out of nowhere, something is not right. What are we meant to make of this sudden dissonance?

Well, one thing to note is that, just as it was God who looked and saw that what he had created was good, it was likewise God who looked and recognised that something was *not* good. Often we can assume the problem was that Adam was lonely. Yet if we pay close attention, we see that the passage doesn't invite us to consider how Adam felt about his aloneness. Unlike the editors of the *Alone* series—who make it very clear how desperately isolated their contestants are feeling—the author of Genesis 2 doesn't say anything at all about how Adam was feeling. The diagnosis comes entirely from Adam's Creator. And that diagnosis is simply that it is not good for him to be alone.

But God's diagnosis doesn't mean that he got to the end of Day 6 and realised he had overlooked something important. Rather, this was God's way of intentionally revealing that he didn't ever intend for the man to be literally the only human being on the planet—that he had designed the man to need a suitable helper.

At this point something interesting happens. Rather than getting straight to it and making Eve, God first parades all the existing living creatures before Adam (v 19). Why? One reason is that it was another teaching moment. Adam didn't instinctively *know* he was alone. He needed to be taught that by recognising that no suitable helper could be found for him (v 20). The parade was also God's way of making it clear to Adam (and all the other creatures) that the special problem of Adam's aloneness required a special solution—Eve.

But God didn't go ahead and create Eve in the same way he had created Adam (that is, from the dust). Rather, he made Eve from the man's very side. God's solution is not to create something entirely new and different to the man—Eve is quite literally bone of his bones and flesh of his flesh (v 23). She is not only a suitable helper fit for him, but she is a suitable helper who is one with him.

If we read Genesis 2:18 carefully, we discover that, in the words of one of my favourite children's books, Adam was not having a "terrible, horrible, not good, very bad day" simply because he was unmarried. No, Adam was quite simply the *only human person in creation*. God taught him, and all the rest of creation with him, that this was not the end plan. The man was not ever meant to be, let alone to stay, alone.

But Adam didn't just need anything. He specifically needed Eve. Why? Well, we find the answer to that question back in the previous chapter.

> *So God created mankind in his own image,*
> *in the image of God he created them;*
> *male and female he created them. (Genesis 1:27)*

It was always God's intention to make humanity in his image as a differentiated *them*—as male and female. They were made to be the same as each other but also different to each other. Here, at the very beginning of all things, we see that God made the man and the woman to be as one, but also to be more than just one. Human beings were not made to be human alone. We were made to be human together.

Marriage Is Only Part of the Answer

All this is why marriage between the man and the woman is right there on view in Genesis:

> *The man said, "This is now bone of my bones and flesh of*
> *my flesh; she shall be called 'woman', for she was taken*
> *out of man." That is why a man leaves his father and*
> *mother and is united to his wife, and they become one*
> *flesh. (2:23-24)*

God created marriage as one human relationship in which men and women were to live and love together—to not be alone. We should not doubt that at all. And yet, God's generous solution to Adam's aloneness was not the meagre provision of just one relationship. He didn't say, *Because you've now got each other, you've got all you and this world will ever need.* Instead he said, "Be fruitful and increase in number; fill the earth and subdue it!" (Genesis 1:28). God's creation of the marriage relationship between Adam and Eve was intended to result in the abundant provision of a multiplicity of relationships. God took someone who was really and truly alone, and then he generated the entire network of human relationships from his very body!

And this is what we observe as we read on in Genesis (and indeed, the rest of Scripture). Adam and his male descendants weren't simply made to be husbands and lovers to women, but also their fathers, grandfathers, uncles, brothers, kin, neighbours, work colleagues and friends. Eve and her female descendants weren't simply made to be wives and lovers to men, but also their mothers, grandmothers, aunts, sisters, kin, neighbours, work colleagues and friends. God created men to relate to women. He created women to relate to men. He created men to relate to other men, and women to relate to other women.

In other words, God's solution to Adam's aloneness was to create an immense wealth of relationships that demonstrate companionship, friendship, community, collegiality, intimacy, togetherness and love in both our sameness (we are all human) and our difference (some of us are male, and some of us are female). He created a vast multitude of people to bear and be his image in the world and to rule over it under him. He created humanity to be together, rather than to be alone.

God was kind enough to bring this magnificent truth home to me even as I was writing this very chapter. Much of this book was written while I was on a solo writing retreat in a little Australian country town. One morning, I needed a change of scenery as I wrote, and so I headed out to a local café. After ordering my chai, I looked around and saw that I could sit at a little table in a dark and cold corner, or I could take a seat at a long communal table drenched in sunlight. I headed straight for the latter. No sooner had I taken a seat than half a dozen other customers appeared in the café. This group of men and women were clearly all friends, and after they placed their orders they asked if they could join me at the table in the sunshine. So there I sat, writing about God's generosity in providing humans with an abundance of relationships, all while watching these men and women delight in each other's company. I looked on, and I saw just how very good it was.

Marriage is fundamental to the creation of human community. But it is not the entirety of it. Marriage is central to the relationships between men and women. But it is not the sum total of them. Marriage is pivotal in God's earthly intentions for his image-bearers. But its purpose is to serve ends greater than itself—both in this creation and in the creation to come. Marriage was only *part* of God's solution to Adam's aloneness. And this means there is much, much more to human relationships than marriage alone.

What's more, we have already seen that this one good type of human relationship has an expiry date! In the life to come, we will have a fullness and depth of relationship with each other beyond anything we can imagine here and now. There, we will be part of a multitude of people, from every place and every time, standing shoulder to shoulder before the throne of God. We will be the definitive opposite of "alone". And yet there, not one of us will be another person's husband or wife. We will be single ever after.

This eternal truth has something very important to impart to us about life in the present. It teaches us that *being unmarried is not the same thing as being alone.*

The Difference Between One-Fleshness and Oneness

A little while ago I heard a pastor share an anecdote about an elderly married couple. They were visiting a new doctor for the first time and giving her their rather extensive medical histories. When the husband began talking about the time when he had had his appendix removed, the wife interjected: "No dear! You didn't have your appendix out. That wasn't you! It was me!". The pastor said that this is what marriage ought to be like—a union in which the two parties are so co-mingled that they forget where one ends and the other begins.

So often we Christians hold marriage out to be the *ultimate* experience of relational oneness, where true "not-aloneness" is to be found. And so, by implication, those not part of such a union are like a pre-Eve Adam, doomed to perpetual aloneness. Singleness becomes tragic because it is seen to be the absence of that ultimate co-mingling.

But Jesus speaks about a different oneness that ought to *really* matter to us Christians. Right before he was arrested, in the presence of his disciples, he prayed for the following:

> *My prayer is not for them alone. I pray also for those who will believe in me through their message, that all of them may be one, Father, just as you are in me and I am in you. May they also be in us so that the world may believe that you have sent me. I have given them the glory that you gave me, that they may be one as we are one—I in them and you in me—so that they may be brought to complete unity. Then the world will know that you sent me and have loved them even as you have loved me.*
>
> (John 17:20-23)

What is the oneness—the opposite to aloneness—that Jesus prays his followers will know? He does not pray for the one-fleshness of marriage, good as that may be. Instead, he asks his Father to grant to his followers the oneness that comes through believing in him. Our Saviour prays that we, his disciples, will know a oneness that echoes the closeness of his relationship with the Father. He prays that we may be brought to the oneness of complete unity—and that this oneness would enable the watching world to know that God sent Jesus into the world for the sake of love.

Can you imagine the impact it would have if church communities rejoiced in the oneness of being his disciples nearly as much as we rejoice in the one-fleshness of being married? Can you imagine what a difference it would make if we were to see the church (not marriage) as the place where none of us are ever alone? Can you imagine how God might use *that* to testify of his love to the watching world?

Singleness Is Not Another Word for Aloneness

Communio's study concludes that the reason why unmarried churchgoers experience much higher rates of loneliness is because they are single. It says that marriage is "an essential relationship to construct a happy and successful life".[7]

But as we have just seen, God's word says that while marriage is *an* answer to human aloneness (at least in this creation), it is not *the* answer. Marriage is *an* expression of relational intimacy, but it is not *the* expression. Marriage is *a* way in which men and women image God in this world but it is not the *only* or even primary way they do that.

Singleness should never be another word for loneliness within the community of God's people: those who Jesus prayed would be one. Contrary to popular Christian opinion today, the tragedy is not singleness itself. No, the real tragedy is that many of our church communities are places in which those who are single experience chronically higher levels of loneliness and relational isolation... simply because they are single.

Whether single or married, we are all part of the same body of Christ, co-heirs of the same gospel promises, brothers and sisters in the same family, and beneficiaries of Jesus' oneness prayer. Because the gospel is very, very good news, not a single one of us is ever alone.

And yet, how does that truth change things for Liz, who intentionally arrives late to church so that she doesn't feel so alone? Or Steven and his kids, who rarely get included in the plans of others? Or Kelly, whom nobody was willing to pray with during church? Well, read on—because that is what we will now turn to consider.

All by Myself

Part 2: Living It Out

It's one thing to believe the Bible's teaching that those who trust in Jesus are never alone. But it's another thing to not actually *feel* lonely. Likewise, as much as we may believe that the church is meant to be the place where Christian men and women feel a deep sense of "oneness", we may still struggle with feelings of relational isolation at church. What do we do with this disconnect between what we believe and what we feel?

Well, in one sense the answer is simple. If we truly believe that those in Christ are never truly alone, then we need to keep preaching that truth to ourselves and each other, over and over and over again—especially when we don't *feel* it to be true. The same Jesus Christ whom we will one day see face to face has promised us that he is with us right here and right now, even to the very end of the age (Matthew 28:20). The more we remind ourselves of Jesus' presence in our lives, the more that truth will shape our thinking and, just as importantly, our feelings.

And because we know that Jesus has prayed that we will be at one with each other, then we can (and should!)

join our prayer with his. So, we pray that our heavenly Father will answer our Saviour's prayer for us, while also praying that he will make *us* the answer to the same prayer of others. And then we eagerly look out for the ways in which he answers those prayers. Let's not allow those moments in which we feel deep unity and solidarity with others in Christ to pass us by. Let's recognise those moments for the joy they are, seek them out and delight in them!

Of course, the flip side is that when we feel let down by others within our church, or disconnected and isolated from them, we need to practise patient perseverance in the face of our disappointment. As we reflect on the forgiveness we have in Christ, we ought to ask God to help us extend forgiveness to those who hurt us. As we rest in the proactive love of God towards us, we should ask him to help us proactively love others, even when—perhaps especially when—we feel overlooked or abandoned.

Putting the Bible's truth about aloneness and togetherness into action means all these things. But it also means some specific things in singleness and in marriage.

Single Christians Are Not Alone

God desires that we singles would know and experience abundant love, intimacy and relational connection in our church families. I know how much it hurts when we don't. Like Liz, I too have been known to time a slightly late arrival at church so as not to feel quite so alone when I walk in the door. I know what it is like to feel both entirely invisible and utterly conspicuous while trying to find a conversation partner over morning tea. I know what it is like to feel very vulnerable in these and other ways. I also know how easy it is to give in to disillusionment—and even to feel self-righteous about it.

What is infinitely harder but also infinitely more precious is imitating Jesus—who loved others deeply, even when they left him feeling unloved.

Jesus has prayed that we would know the same depth of oneness with our brothers and sisters in Christ that he knows with his Father. So please, don't throw in the towel on that! Yes, it can be really hard to go to church each week when we know that we'll be walking in (and out) alone. But if we don't go, then how will we *ever* experience the oneness Jesus wants for his people? Yes, it can feel very exposing to approach a group of people after church to join in a conversation. But if we don't ever do that, then how will we allow ourselves to know and be known by others?

My friend Jo didn't get married until well into her forties. She told me that for many years before that, she'd experienced a sense of automatic exclusion from conversations with married friends after church. She'd often be gently rebuffed with a "Sorry, we're talking about stroller choices. Boring!" When that happened, Jo would gently remind them that as someone of the same age as them, she had nieces, nephews and many friends with kids and so, "Yes, I had some thoughts about stroller choices! But even if I didn't, I was just happy to be there with them, part of the conversation." Jo told me that expressing that tended to nip exclusion in the bud fairly quickly.

Of course, there are also plenty of other topics beyond stroller choices that we single Christians are not only able to participate in but actively foster. Not long ago, Claire, a single friend of mine at church, asked a few of us if there was something from the previous week that we were particularly thankful to God for. Because post-church conversations *do* often tend to veer towards the mundane things of life such as stroller choices and the latest shows we've been watching, I was a little discombobulated at first!

But it turned into a beautiful moment of shared spiritual reflection. It fostered a genuine sense of togetherness. Perhaps you could attempt to initiate these kinds of conversations after church this week.

As single members of Jesus' body, let's not settle for feeling alone and lonely amid our spiritual family. Sometimes this will involve us taking the (repeated) initiative to get to know others and asking how we can walk alongside them. Other times it will involve us being brave and communicating with others how they can get to know us and walk alongside us. But the more we model this, the more others will imitate it. The more we are part of the change, the more change we'll begin to see happening around us. The oneness that Jesus has prayed we will know is indeed worth knowing!

Of course, this shouldn't just be limited to relationships with those in our church. There are plenty of other times when those of us who are single struggle with a sense of loneliness, and so there are plenty of other opportunities for us to pray for and pursue more relational togetherness with other Christians (and indeed, with non-Christians).

I often find holidays (vacations, for my North American friends) one of the toughest aspects of single life. I know that spending all my downtime by myself is not good for me. But it can be hard to align my schedule with those of other single friends. And even if there are times when we are able to make our schedules work, that doesn't automatically mean we would holiday well together! And so, I spent years looking at my married friends' social-media holiday snaps with envy, wishing I was there with them. But what I didn't realise is that my married friends had no idea I was feeling that way. For them, contemplating a holiday without kids was like dreaming the impossible dream! They couldn't fathom that someone would actually *want* to go on a break with their horde. But once they knew I was up for it, the invitations started rolling in. Mere wishful thinking or dropping little relational breadcrumbs is bound to end in disappointment. Enjoying relationships with others involves active communication and vulnerability.

And while we are on the topic of children, a word about those too. Children are a wonderful blessing from God. And yet, unfortunately, in many Christian circles today, the conversation around this has morphed into an obsession with fertility. Married couples who cannot have children can be particular casualties of such an obsession. But so, too, can many unmarried Christians.

If you are a single Christian who longs to have children of your own, remember that you are longing for a truly good thing. So bring that longing to God in prayerful supplication. Pour out the desires and anxieties of your heart, knowing that you have a heavenly Father who loves you deeply.

But, please, resist the lure of a world—and, too often, some churches—that commodifies children into little beings who we (perhaps artificially) create to give ourselves a sense of relational fulfilment. Having children is a great joy, but God has intended that great joy to be a fruit of marriage, not an outlet to meet our perceived need for completion. His design is for children to experience the love and care of a mother and a father, not to be generated so that a woman or man might know what it is like to be loved and cared for by a child.

I know those can be very hard words to hear, especially if you are a single Christian who desperately longs to have a child of your own. Moreover, the older I get as a childless single woman, the more I am aware of the implications of that for my future, especially in old age. The anxiety and sadness are real.

But there are many ways in which your life can be deeply enriched through relationships with (other people's) children. Even more importantly, there are ways in which you can love vulnerable children who *desperately* need care and compassion. I live in stunned admiration of my unmarried friend Gemma, who resigned from her job so that she could become a full-time foster mother to young babies. She welcomes these precious little ones into her life, all while others work with their biological parents in the hopes of seeing their family reunified. Gemma joyfully—and sacrificially—embraces the opportunities she has to be a parent to these vulnerable children, even if only for a little while.

So, friend, don't buy into any sort of Christian nonsense that paints your singleness as a tragedy or says that you are alone because you don't have a spouse. You were not made solely to have a husband or a wife; you were made to live in relationships with others. And in Christ you have an utter abundance of those! After all, he promises that in him we will "receive a hundred times as much [as] *in this present age*: homes, brothers, sisters, mothers, children" (Mark 10:30). Because he is not a liar, don't settle for feeling alone and lonely. Your life is intended to testify to the abundant intimacy, deep togetherness and beautiful oneness that we were created to crave here and now, and designed to delight in for all eternity. Actively pursue that oneness!

Married Christians Need More Than Marriage Alone

If you are married, then your relationship with your spouse is a wonderfully good thing. But it should not be your everything. You, too, were created to love and be loved by a myriad of different people. So don't expect your spouse to meet all of your relational needs or to be the one who stops you from ever feeling lonely again. Both of you need other people to love and be loved by. Both of you need other people to know and be known by.

This is a particularly important truth for married men to hear and apply. I was recently talking to someone whose mother died about four years ago. After decades of marriage, her father is single again. And now, he finds himself relationally isolated. When he was married, he had cultivated no real friendships of his own. His daughter told me that he had only been friends with other men because those men were married to women who were friends with his wife. Now, all those couples remain couple-friends, but he is no longer part of a couple and so no longer part of them. He doesn't know how to be friends as a single man, and they don't know how to befriend him as a single man. His is a very common story.

If you are married, don't smother your marriage by only relating to others through it. Rather, strengthen and fuel your marriage by allowing it to breathe in the oxygen of other important relationships in your life. Actively seek out the oneness that Jesus has prayed you will know with others within his body.

Of course, the perfect way to do that is by proactively investing in relationships and friendship with others at your church... and not just with those who are like you. This will entail moving out of your comfort zone and meeting new people. One particular way you could do this is by not always sitting with your spouse every week in church. It's certainly not wrong to sit next to your husband or wife! But what might it communicate about the togetherness we have in the church if, every second or third week, your nuclear family decided to sit with different members of your spiritual family?

Or perhaps you could seek out different people who attend church alone and invite them to sit with your family each week. Or, if you arrive at church and see someone sitting by themselves, why not ask if it is okay for you all to sit next to them? Or maybe you could give a single friend a lift to church occasionally so that they don't always arrive alone—or arrange to meet them outside the church so they have someone to walk through the church doors with.

If you need to go and pick up your kids from the children's programme as soon as the service is over, why not invite a couple of your single friends to come with you so that they are not left looking for someone to talk to? And in conversations, please don't assume your single friends are disinterested in the mundanity of your married lives or that they don't have anything contribute to that discussion.

Pursuing this kind of togetherness is not only a way to love your unmarried Christian friends—though it certainly is that! It is also a way for you to experience the kind of relational blessings God intends them to be for you. In Jesus, we have been adopted into a spiritual family of countless brothers and sisters.

It was not good for the man to be alone. And so praise God that, single or married, those of us who belong to his family will never again be alone.

The Wind Beneath
My Wings

Part 1: Unwrapping the Gift of Singleness

By the time I turned 20, I was an expert gift-wrapper. I learnt my trade working from in a boutique department store and not long after found myself teaching creative gift-wrapping courses and providing a Christmas gift-wrapping service at a luxury shopping centre. The gift-wrapping world was my oyster! However, I soon realised that your most impressive skill can quickly become your greatest liability. For years, family and friends "persuaded" me into wrapping every single one of their Christmas, birthday, thank-you, engagement, wedding and baby-shower presents. Eventually, I feigned irreversible finger damage from all that ribbon curling and retired from the field for good. I now keep a steady supply of gift bags on hand.

The magic of gift wrapping is that it takes an object— even one that is seemingly mundane—and elevates it to an offering of significance, value and even love. This is as true of a pair of socks as it is of a crystal vase.

It is also true of singleness, at least in the church's estimation.

It's a fair bet that any single Christian beyond the bloom of young adulthood will be familiar with the phrase "the gift of singleness". Books, articles and sermons on singleness (and marriage) often refer to it as a kind of self-evident reality.

The same single Christian may also find themselves the subject of conversation—or, more frequently, speculation—about whether or not they have been "gifted" for singleness. The 25-year-old single man who has never been in a long-term relationship is quizzed about whether he has "the gift" or is, instead, a commitment phobe. The 37-year-old unmarried woman who longs to be a wife wonders where her "gift" has gone, even as the older ladies at church are eager to assure her that "there is a man out there for you yet, my dear!" Perhaps the 50-year-old active on every ministry roster at your church is looked on approvingly for putting their "gift of singleness" to good use. At the same time, their counterpart whose life circumstances don't offer them the same level of flexibility is seen to be squandering theirs.

You can scarcely mention singleness in the Christian community without bumping into the (so-called) "gift of singleness" or, more recently, the "gift of celibacy" (more on that in a later chapter). And yet, when we search the Bible for that phrase, we're left scratching our heads. It's just not there. So what exactly is it? And why does it feature so prominently in Christian discussions about the unmarried life?

Well, "the gift of singleness" (which I'll now interchangeably refer to as "the gift") is a kind of short-hand way of summarising these words from the apostle Paul:

*I wish that all of you were as I am. But each of you has
your own gift from God; one has this gift, another has
that. Now to the unmarried and the widows I say: it is
good for them to stay unmarried, as I do.*
(1 Corinthians 7:7-8)

From these two brief verses, we have built a whole system,
indeed a whole theology, of what it means (or does not
mean) to be "legitimately" single as a Christian. But if we
scratch beneath the surface, we soon discover that our
usual understanding of singleness as a gift leaves much to
be desired. To understand why this is the case, we need to
explore the assumptions that have become built into our
thinking about the gift.

To do that, I'm going to have to speak fairly generally.
As such, not all of what follows may precisely represent
what you—or perhaps someone you know—mean by the
phrase. My aim is to give a broad-brush impression of
what is commonly meant in discussions about the gift of
singleness today.

How Would You Like Your Singleness Gift-Wrapped?

SPIRITUAL
First of all, we usually assume the gift is a spiritual gift—
that is, a special empowerment of the Holy Spirit for a
particular purpose. In this case, the gift is seen to spiritually
empower the unmarried Christian in two extraordinary
ways: 1) through a supernatural freedom from sexual desire,
temptation or longing and 2) through a supernatural sense
of contentment with or happiness in their singleness. These
two empowerments are typically seen to go hand in hand.

Without this spiritual empowerment, the unmarried
Christian is often thought not capable of living a fully
faithful and faithfully fulfilled life. Indeed, lacking the

necessary gift means it may be dangerous, even deviant, for them to try. And so, the gift is essentially thought to be the special ability God gives certain people to be A-okay with not being married. It also allows the rest of us to be A-okay with them not being married.

And yet, when we read 1 Corinthians 7, we discover that there is no mention of the Spirit in that chapter at all, and certainly not in connection to the gifts (yes, plural) mentioned in verses 7-8. There, Paul just uses the common Greek word that we translate as gift (or elsewhere, grace) with no spiritual-like adjectives attached.

So, where does the assumed spiritual character of the gift come into it? Well, it is borrowed from what Paul says a bit later in his letter. In 1 Corinthians 12 and 14, Paul writes about the gifts of healing, prophecy, tongues, miracles and so on. He says that those who do these remarkable things are spiritually empowered for them by God. These are indeed "spiritual gifts".

And so, when we come across the spiritual gifts of chapters 12 and 14, the language clicks with us: "Hang on, didn't Paul say something about gifts back in chapter 7?" We read the gifts of those later chapters back into chapter 7, deciding that the "gift of singleness" must be just like those gifts in chapters 12 and 14—a special spiritual gift received as an extraordinary empowerment from God. In other words, it becomes not so much the gift of singleness, but the gift *for* singleness. We think of it as a kind of additional booster shot or top-up of the Holy Spirit that the godly and contented single Christian needs *in order to be* godly and contented. Essentially, it is the wind beneath the single Christian's wings!

LIFELONG

A second assumption we make about the gift is that it

has been given for life. If the gift is as described above, we assume it would be both capricious and cruel of God to empower the long-term single person with a gift that has only a limited lifespan. How could they be expected to remain godly and content in their singleness if the empowering gift has an expiry date attached to it?

By the same logic, we reason that it would be terribly ungrateful and churlish for the "gifted" single Christian to decide at some point that they'd rather trade in their God-given gift of singleness for one of marriage. The "gift of singleness" isn't the type of gift that can be sent back for a refund or exchange—at least, not without deeply offending, perhaps even sinning against, the gift giver.

For these reasons, we typically think that the special spiritual empowerment to singleness is also a *permanent* empowerment to singleness.

SUBJECTIVE

In the usual course of things, the giver's motive and the action of their giving are what make it clear that something is indeed a gift. However, things aren't quite so clear-cut when it comes to the "gift of singleness". Indeed, this particular gift isn't seen to be so much about the giver and their motives as it is about the receiver and their feelings. You see, we generally hold that it is single people *themselves* who are best able to decide whether or not they've been gifted with singleness. And the way they can decide this is by looking within. The author C. Peter Wagner explains it like this:

> *If you are single and **know down in your heart** that you would get married in an instant if a reasonable opportunity presented itself, you probably don't have the gift of celibacy. If you are single and **find yourself terribly frustrated** by unfulfilled sexual impulses, you*

probably don't have the gift. But if neither of these things
seems to bother you—*rejoice—you may have found one*
of your spiritual gifts.[8]

In other words, it is up to the unmarried individual to
determine whether or not they have been given the gift.
Furthermore, it's *their* desires, their longings and the
things they find themselves bothered (or unbothered) by
that is the deciding factor on that count. If being single
is something the person wants, then they should rejoice!
They've been given that gift by God. But if they don't
want to be single, they clearly haven't received the gift and
should be setting their sights on marriage instead.

RARE AND EXCEPTIONAL
Our final assumption about the gift concerns its rarity and
consequently its perceived value. Whenever something is
available to only a few people—like private box tickets to
a Taylor Swift concert—the value of that thing increases
dramatically. If anyone and everyone were given access to
that very exclusive opportunity, nobody would really prize
it. It would lose a lot of its value.

Likewise, seeing the gift of singleness as a special
spiritual booster shot that God gives to only a very small
number of special individuals means that the gift's value
goes up in our estimation. Naturally, this also means that
the gift recipient also goes up in our estimation—they
begin to take on a kind of rarefied aura.

Where Did My Gift Go?
With all that being said, here's my attempt to summarise
what many Christians today usually think about the
(so-called) "gift of singleness". We typically believe that
the "gift of singleness" is an extraordinary spiritual
empowerment that God gives to a few special individuals. It

is a rare booster shot of sexual self-discipline and personal satisfaction with singleness. This spiritual "topping up" is necessary if an unmarried Christian is to enjoy long-term holiness and happiness. An unmarried Christian knows whether or not they have received the gift based on their inner feelings of conviction and contentment about being and remaining single.

Those singles who don't strongly desire to be married can take comfort, even rejoice, in the idea that they have been given this special divine gift. It provides them with an explanation as to why they experience their singleness as a positive thing. It also provides others with a reason to consider their singleness as a positive thing.

But this understanding of the gift leaves the majority of single (and single-again) Christians in somewhat of a no-man's land. Their earnest desire to be married and/or their experience of sexual desire and temptation suggests that God has not given them the gift. However, he has also not gifted them with marriage.

And so, they wonder why a loving God would withhold *both* of these things from them? Or perhaps it is not God's goodness that is in doubt but his power—maybe God's hands are tied, and he *cannot* give one or the other to them? And so, if they wish to get married (and, since they don't have the gift, they are told they should), it looks as if it's up to them to make that happen. This often leads the single Christian to become ever more consumed with the search for a spouse and ever more willing to compromise on the kinds of qualities they ought to be looking for in one.

Do you see how our understanding of the gift is ultimately about far more than just what we think about singleness itself? It takes us to the heart of who we think God is and how we think he is (or is not) active in our lives. It's for this reason that we need to peel back the wrapping paper and take a much closer look at the good gift contained within.

Peeling Back the Wrapping

To start with, let's consider the implications of seeing the gift as a necessary booster shot of spiritual self-control.[9] Because here's the thing: if we believe that the unmarried Christian requires an additional spiritual empowerment to live with self-control, contentment and godliness, then what we are *really* saying is that they need something more than what Scripture says all Christians have already been given in Christ.

> *For the grace of God has appeared that offers salvation to all people. It teaches us to say "No" to ungodliness and worldly passions, and to live self-controlled, upright and godly lives in this present age, while we wait for the blessed hope—the appearing of the glory of our great God and Saviour, Jesus Christ, who gave himself for us to redeem us from all wickedness and to purify for himself a people that are his very own, eager to do what is good.*
> *(Titus 2:11-14)*

To put it bluntly, our understanding of the gift insists that the unmarried Christian needs something *more* than the "ordinary" grace of God to live a life of godly faithfulness to Christ. But this puts Paul's words in 1 Corinthians 7:7-8 in direct opposition to his words in Titus 2:11-14. It diminishes, even undermines, the extraordinary and extraordinarily powerful grace of God given to every believer.

But wait, there's more. Consider also these other words from the apostle Paul:

> *But the fruit of the Spirit is love, joy, peace, forbearance, kindness, goodness, faithfulness, gentleness and self-*

control. Against such things there is no law. Those who belong to Christ Jesus have crucified the flesh with its passions and desires. Since we live by the Spirit, let us keep in step with the Spirit. (Galatians 5:22-25)

Our typical understanding of the gift says that the Holy Spirit's "ordinary" fruitful work is not enough for singles to crucify the flesh and bear the spiritual fruit of self-control. It implies they need *more* of the Holy Spirit—an additional topping up—than their married counterparts. They need the extra "gift" because the "ordinary" dose they received isn't capable of bearing enough self-control for their situation. Surely this cannot be true?

But even if we *were* somehow able to reconcile ourselves to the idea that living as a sexually faithful unmarried person requires an additional booster shot of the Holy Spirit, why would we think this only applies to sexual sin, and specifically sexual sin in singleness and not marriage? We don't think the Christian person prone to habitual anger or gluttony requires an extra-special dose of spiritual empowerment. So why do we think the unmarried Christian who struggles with sexual temptation does (even as the married Christian with the same struggle apparently doesn't)?

Let's also consider the nature and purpose of spiritual gifts according to the New Testament. Earlier, I suggested that our understanding of the gift relies on us reading Paul's later comments about spiritual gifts in 1 Corinthians 12 and 14 back into chapter 7. But the irony is that in doing that, we fail to recognise the whole thrust of Paul's later discussion of those spiritual gifts—namely, that they are not given for the recipient's benefit, satisfaction or sense of contentment but for "the common good" (12:7). The spiritual gifts listed in those later chapters are given *for the express purpose of building up the church.*

Now compare that with our contemporary notion of the gift of singleness. Certainly, it can have an other-person-centred veneer. We rejoice that the gifted single can be more servant-hearted (normally expressed by their appearing more frequently on the church rosters). But if we scratch beneath the surface, it's clear that we *really* think the main purpose of the gift is to ensure that the single person is both happy and holy in their situation. That is, the gift's usefulness lies in its liberating them from their *personal* struggles with discontentment and persistent longings for marriage. This is precisely why the gift's presence is thought to be determined by the single person's feelings about their singleness.

But determining whether or not we have the gift based on our feelings is a dangerous thing to do. Of course, we should care about our feelings, cultivate them wisely, and recognise their significance in our lives. But we would be foolish to consider them a truly reliable source of discernment. Why? Because our feelings are flawed and fragile. Sin means that we don't always feel rightly, and we don't always feel the right things to the right degree.

Moreover, our feelings change. Who is to say we will still feel the same way about our singleness next week, next year, or in ten years? What happens if my positive feelings change down the track? As Charlotte told me, "I'm in my early twenties and am thankful for my singleness. But will my attitude towards it change over time? Will my contentment turn into a burden?" The perceived subjective nature of the gift leads us towards a lot of potential uncertainty and anxiety.

Lastly, we should consider how our perception of the gift's rarity aligns with Scripture's teaching about the goodness of singleness. In 1 Corinthians 7:7 the apostle Paul says he wishes *everyone* was single as he was. But we typically conclude that the only truly good kind of singleness is exceptionally rare. What accounts for the significant gap between our minimal expectations and the apostle's expansive ideal? Why would a God who delights in giving good gifts to his children (Matthew 7:11; James 1:17) give *this* particular gift so sparingly, even as the divinely inspired apostle Paul says he wishes *all* were unmarried (1 Corinthians 7:7)?

Can you see how, for many, the "gift of singleness" has become a messy mix of thinking about God's character, the work of the Spirit and the power of the gospel? A confusing tangle regarding sin, repentance, redemption, forgiveness, sanctification and godliness? And yet, the problem isn't simply that our thinking is confused and messy. It's that this confusion leads to messy real-life implications for real-life people.

"I do not feel like I have the gift of singleness," Anna wrote. "But as a 41-year-old Christian woman, I also have very minimal dating prospects. And so, I am very angry with God because I have deep desires in my heart which he hasn't provided for, even though he seems to readily meet them for most other people." She continued, "I know in my heart that God is good, but right now, my heart's question is 'Is God good for me?'" Another friend, May, has always deeply desired marriage, but her prayers have remained unanswered. It appears that God has given her neither a spouse nor the gift that would make her content in her singleness. In her words, she feels "abandoned and betrayed by God. I feel like I'm being punished or, at least, that I have been utterly forgotten by him".

This is how so much of the current framing of the (so-called) gift leaves countless Christians feeling. And yet, this is not who our good God is nor how he works for good in our lives! The very gospel itself assures us of God's infinite goodness and his unending power. This means that our contemporary understanding of "the gift of singleness" *cannot be* what the apostle Paul meant in 1 Corinthians 7:7-8.

So what then *did* he mean in those verses? That's what we'll explore next.

The Wind Beneath
My Wings

Part 2: Living It Out

Eliza has always been fairly content in her singleness. Many of her Christian friends (and also church leaders) have told her that she obviously "has the gift". But Eliza wonders what those same people would think if she *did* get married someday. As she and I were chatting about this (hypothetical) scenario, she said she doubted that any of her friends would try to discourage her from letting go of her "gifted" singleness in order to become a wife. But why, she asked? After all, wouldn't her decision to get married be a bit of a slap in the face to God, who had given her such a rare and precious gift? Why wouldn't her friends be concerned about her rejection of God's gift to her? Or perhaps even rebuke her for it?

The truth is that even though we Christians call gifted singleness good, it seems that deep down, we still think that marriage is better. There is an implicit hierarchy between the two in which singleness never comes out on top. Even "gifted" singleness is, in Eliza's words, "little more than a consolation prize until something better (marriage) comes along".

The problem is that this stands in stark contrast to a passage like 1 Corinthians 7, in which the apostle Paul says being unmarried is a genuinely good situation for followers of Christ. Indeed, in verse 38, Paul even suggests it is *better* to remain single than to get married! Even just typing that last sentence made me squirm in my seat—am I allowed to say such a thing?! It is right there in the pages of Scripture, but saying it out loud seems all but impossible. Why is that?

Perhaps it's because, when we compare our lived experiences as single people to those of our married friends, the latter just seems like a better deal. But I also think it's because we humans have such a hard time believing that two alternative things can both be good at the same time. We read Paul calling singleness good, and we bristle because that seems to imply that marriage isn't good.

But that's not what the apostle Paul thinks. It is not what God's word says. You see, 1 Corinthians 7 models a far more nuanced and wonderful way of thinking than simply "this good = that bad". He writes that he wishes all were as he is (i.e. unmarried). But he immediately goes on to say that "each of you has your own gift from God; one has this gift, another has that" (v 7). God has given different gifts to different people. One of those gifts is simply the gift of being single for so long as you are single (or single again). And the other kind of gift—the gift of marriage—is simply the gift of being married for so long as you are married. *And both of these different gifts are both good!*

Here, then, is what "the gift of singleness" really is: simply the gift of being single. Now, if you think this sounds like a rather novel way to interpret Paul's words in 1 Corinthians 7:7-8, let me assure you that it isn't new at all. In fact, this is how the earliest Church Fathers in the 3rd and 4th centuries consistently understood those verses.[10] As we will see in a later chapter, it wasn't until the Reformation that this changed and a new interpretation came to the fore.

Understanding "the gift of singleness" in this way—the gift of being single—means that its goodness lies in the *purposes God has embedded into the single Christian life* and *not* in whether we want the gift or not. It means the gift's value lies in the fact that *God has given singleness to his people as a good thing* and *not* in how we feel about being single, becoming single again or remaining single for ever.

Singleness is not a good gift only to a rare few who seem to have an extraordinary empowerment to contentment. No, it is a good gift for *every* single because God himself has called it good. It's good because God himself has a good purpose for it. It's good because God himself is at work in singleness (as he is in marriage) to remind us that the very best is still yet to come. It's time for us to take the gift of singleness off the shelf, peel back its wrapping paper and delight in the truly good thing that lies within.

If You Are Single, Then You Have the Gift

If you are an unmarried Christian, I'm guessing that you grapple with grieving what isn't and what may never be or what may never be again. Perhaps, like me, you wrestle with godliness and contentment in your chaste singleness. You probably experience seasonal peaks and troughs in how you feel about being unmarried.

As we saw in the last chapter, there are many in the church who would tell us that this is evidence that we have not been given the "gift of singleness"—that if God wanted us to remain single, he would have specially empowered us to be consistently content in it. That if our singleness doesn't feel good *to* us, then it isn't good *for* us.

But have you ever stopped to wonder why married people aren't told that if God wanted them to be married, he'd especially empower them to be consistently content and faithful in their marriage? Have you stopped to consider why we don't say to a husband or wife that if their marriage doesn't feel good to them, then it is no longer good for them?

In fact, we tend to have the *opposite* expectations when it comes to marriage (and rightly so). We readily acknowledge that marriage can be hard. We expect husbands and wives to struggle with contentment and faithfulness. And when they *do* struggle with these things, we don't suggest that perhaps they aren't cut out for marriage after all. We don't automatically conclude that they are clearly not good at being married nor that marriage is not good for them.

As my friend Alex puts it, "Why are singles unfairly held to a higher standard of contentment than our married counterparts? Why is it normal to bemoan the hardships of marriage, while 'real' singles are expected to be perfectly content?". His questions are good ones. Why does being married remain a good situation even when it is hard, but the same does not apply to being unmarried?

Here's the thing: the goodness of your singleness is not dependent on whether you feel good about it. Indeed, your singleness remains a good gift *even when you feel just the opposite about it*. Why? Well, because of the dignity that God has granted it—including that it's a signpost to our relationships as brothers and sisters in the ever after to come (as we saw in chapter 1). This means that your singleness remains a good gift even when you don't experience it as good.

I know that can be difficult to believe. But your heavenly Father has given you everything you need to love him, serve others and grow in Christ-likeness, *even when* you struggle and suffer in your singleness.

> *For the grace of God has appeared that offers salvation to all people. It teaches us to say "No" to ungodliness and worldly passions, and to live self-controlled, upright and godly lives in this present age, while we wait for the blessed hope—the appearing of the glory of our great God and Saviour, Jesus Christ, who gave himself for us to redeem us from all wickedness and to purify for himself a people that are his very own, eager to do what is good.*
> *(Titus 2:11-14)*

God's grace teaches you to resist the temptation to have sex with someone whom you are not married to. God's grace trains you to be self-controlled and upright in your singleness by saying no to watching pornography or lusting after someone in your mind. Jesus Christ gave himself up for you to redeem you from wickedness, to purify you for himself and to make you eager to do what is good. So don't buy the lie that, for your singleness to be good, you need something more than the "ordinary" grace of God!

And don't buy the lie that, if you struggle to enjoy your singleness, you are missing out on the really good stuff of life. According to Jesus, "The thief comes only to steal and kill and destroy; I have come that they may have life, and have it to the full" (John 10:10). Indeed, Jesus laid down *his* life so that *we* might truly have life. And not just any sort of life—rather, life to the max!

Yes, we can find aspects of our singleness consistently hard and perhaps even deeply painful. Yes, many of us feel deep grief at not being a husband or a wife and lament over not having the joy of being a mother or a father. But that does not mean we are living half a life. No! The life Jesus has given us here and now is overflowing with abundance. The eternal life he has promised us—one in which, in our relationships with each other, we will all be "single ever after"—will be abundant beyond what we can even imagine. So don't buy the lie that your singleness means you are living a substandard Christian life. You're not.

Of course, none of this means that any disappointment, hurt or pain we feel in our singleness is illegitimate.

It doesn't mean that we just need to pull up our socks and get over it.

It doesn't mean that we shouldn't ask others to love us in ways that brings hope and healing to those hurts.

It doesn't even mean that we shouldn't pray that God might give us another good gift: that of marriage.

But it does mean that we will regularly remind ourselves that God has not overlooked or abandoned us.

It does mean that we consistently preach to ourselves that God has given us something that is good and precious and valuable *in his sight*.

It does mean that we prayerfully reshape our vision of our singleness around his—seeking to realign our singleness with his purposes for it and to honour and value our singleness as he does.

James writes, "Every good and perfect gift is from above, coming down from the Father of the heavenly lights, who does not change like shifting shadows" (James 1:17). Your singleness *is* a good gift from your constantly good heavenly Father. Will you receive it as such?

If You Are Married or a Pastor (or Both!), You Need to Understand the Gift Too

If you are married, then you are called to walk alongside, build up and help carry the burdens of your single brothers and sisters in Christ. This means that how you think about and respond to their singleness as "gift" is very important. If you pastor a church, then you pastor a flock that includes a range of single Christians who have been entrusted to your care. This means that your thinking and preaching about and applications for singleness as "gift" are very important.

It may be that you've only ever understood the gift(s) in 1 Corinthians 7:7-8 in exactly the way I've suggested above—namely, that the situations of being single or married are both good gifts from God. If that is the case, then I'm deeply encouraged!

And yet, it is likely that other married people will be less thoughtful about what those verses mean and so less considerate about how they engage with their single friends. And if you are a pastor, it is very probable that some members of your flock won't be as clear about what those verses mean—especially because social media and the internet mean that yours is not the only influential voice they will be hearing. All of this can have troubling real-life implications for single Christians.

I recently met a Christian woman named Heidi. She is in her late thirties, has always longed to be a wife and a mother, and has consistently prayed that God would grant her those things. Heidi told me of the time when she had two back-to-back conversations after church one morning. In the first, a married friend suggested Heidi clearly didn't have "the gift", was being too passive in her singleness, and challenged her to be more intentional in pursuing marriage. She encouraged Heidi to sign up again for online dating and to "not be so picky this time around". In the very next conversation, a different married friend gently rebuked Heidi for idolising marriage and suggested that only when she stopped being so focused on finding a husband would God answer her prayers and give her one.

Well intended as these comments were, they left Heidi bewildered and hurt. Her friends demonstrated a very confused understanding of God's loving and gracious character. They even encouraged Heidi towards a works-based mentality in which, if she just did the right things in the right way, she would prove herself worthy of God answering her prayers. In an effort to avoid these kinds of painful conversations, Heidi now rarely speaks with married members of her church about her longing for marriage.

If you are a married Christian, let me encourage you to take stock of how you think and talk about the singleness of your unmarried friends. Do you see it as either an exceptional superpower or, alternatively, a tragic problem to be solved? Could it perhaps lie somewhere in between those two poles—namely, a God-given situation in which your single friends experience both joy and grief? To that point, do you *know* how they experience it? Have you asked them? For example, your instinct to match-make may be well intended, but have you actually checked if this is something they want? Your sadness that they haven't found "their one" may be genuinely felt, but do you know them well enough to know if they truly are sad and what shape that sadness takes?

Moreover, do you intentionally love them in the midst of their singleness? For example, do you look out for the moments of joy and reasons for celebration in their lives, or do those things pass by unnoticed and unremarked? How you can practically meet them where they are in both their sadness and their joy? As one single Christian person said to me, "It's not enough for my married friends to tell me to 'just be content in Jesus', when they don't lift a finger to do what Jesus cannot do for me right now—to give me a hug, to talk to me over a meal, to look after me when I'm poorly, to advocate for me when I can't speak for myself. I need them to not only help me see that my singleness is good but to help me experience my singleness as good."

If you are a pastor, let me encourage you to take stock of how you think and teach about singleness in your church or, more to the point, the *actual single people* in your church. If I asked you to spontaneously list off their names, how complete would that list be? Would all the widowed and divorced members of your flock readily make it on? What about the single parents? Do you see and know the singles under your pastoral care? How often are your sermons full of marriage and family illustrations but little else? How frequently do you celebrate something other than engagements, marriages and babies at church? What you communicate and model is vital to the pastoral well-being of single Christians within your church, as well as essential in equipping their married brothers and sisters to love them in their singleness.

My prayer—and, I hope, yours—is that your church would increasingly be a place where single brothers and sisters know that both marriage *and singleness* are truly good gifts from our truly good God.

4

It's My Life

Part 1: The Complexity of Choice and Circumstance

"I remember a day when the preacher spoke about 'chosen singleness' as some sort of awesome and admiration-worthy state of holiness and brilliance," Kat recounted to me. "As someone who was single but had always wanted to be married, it left me feeling worthless for not being one of these holy saints who had 'chosen' to be single".

In our last chapter, we saw that the spiritual empowerment understanding of the "gift of singleness" leaves many unmarried Christians feeling forgotten by God or doubtful of his goodness and sovereignty. But this is not the only thing that can leave them feeling adrift. So too can the increasingly common idea that the singleness of those who intentionally and purposefully choose to remain unmarried is superior to that of people who, like Kat, would choose to marry if they could.

Choosing to Say "I Will"

In her excellent book *Marriage, a History*, Stephanie Coontz observes how, for "thousands of years, people had little choice about whether and whom to marry".[11] Marriage was primarily a coming together of families, based around social, political and economic considerations. But over the last couple of centuries, marriage in the West has come to almost entirely reflect the autonomous choice of the guy in the suit and the girl in the white dress, who make their decision based on what they hope will bring them the most emotional fulfilment and personal happiness. This development is not an altogether bad one. However, it is rather new, and its emphasis on the importance of choice for personal fulfilment leaves us in a bit of a quandary when it comes to that thing that isn't marriage—singleness.

We all know single Christians who would choose to marry if the choice was theirs. Indeed, perhaps you are one such a single person. Even some who feel generally content in their singleness are still open to the possibility of marriage. And yet, for many, that possibility never seems to present itself. No matter how many social mixers they attend, online dating apps they try out, matchmaking friends they have and earnest prayers they offer, marriage seems to remain out of their reach. And so the concept of having control over their own marital destiny feels little more than an abstract ideal.

The frustration they feel is further compounded by a surrounding culture that heavily idealises choice as necessary for personal fulfilment and authenticity. That is, the world around Kat insists that, if she is to be the author of her own life, she needs to be utterly free to enact any choice she so desires. In the words of the great Jon Bon Jovi, "It's My Life".

This can leave many singles not only grieving for what seems beyond their reach but feeling as if they are victims of their circumstances—as though their life is not actually theirs after all. What is more, because we Christians are more influenced by that worldly veneration of choice than we realise, many within the church today are increasingly doubtful that singleness can truly be good for a person—or perhaps more to the point, truly useful for the kingdom—unless it is has been actively chosen and intentionally stepped into.

Intentional Singles Only Need Apply?

An example of this is found in a 2023 article, "Singleness in the New Covenant" by professor of theology Stephen Wellum. While his article is not primarily focused on distinguishing between actively chosen singleness and its non-intentional counterpart, the distinction is very important to it nonetheless. Wellum argues that Christian singleness has a unique significance in the now-but-not-yet—to which I say a hearty "Amen!" However, he quickly clarifies that he only holds this to be true for *intentional* singleness.[12] But what exactly does he mean by intentional singleness? Helpfully, he provides us with a clear definition:

> *I use the language of "intentional singleness" to reflect the unconstrained deliberate choice made by a single person in 1 Corinthians 7:37 to remain single for the Lord's sake, in contrast to those who would like to marry but never have the opportunity for a variety of reasons.[13]*

In other words, intentional singleness is proactively chosen singleness (presumably for life). It sets apart the person who has made an "unconstrained deliberate choice" to remain unmarried from someone who would choose to marry if the opportunity arose (those we might call "incidental" or "circumstantial" singles). It is also freely chosen "for the Lord's sake". That is, the person who voluntarily chooses to remain unmarried does so because they believe it allows them to dedicate themselves to the Lord—often in a way, or to a degree, that distinguishes them from and perhaps even above other single Christians. You might also hear this referred to as "vocational singleness".

Wellum is certainly not alone in making this hierarchical distinction between different types of singleness. In fact, to see this in action, we need only look at how the vocabulary about the unmarried life has begun to change over the last decade or so. When I commenced my doctoral research back in 2016, the umbrella term that was almost universally used to refer to the situation of an unmarried Christian was "singleness". Now, less than ten years later, another term—"celibacy"—is taking centre stage.

You may have noticed this changing vocabulary—or perhaps you will now that I have drawn your attention to it. It is becoming very common to see Christian leaders, writers, pastors and other influential figures speaking of "celibacy" rather than "singleness". For example, I was excited to see that a 2020 book, *Sanctified Sexuality*, included two chapters on singleness from two different authors. Great! A book on sexuality that doesn't sideline unmarried Christians! But I soon discovered that in those chapters, titled "Celibacy According to Jesus and Paul" and "Celibacy and the Gospel", both authors focused exclusively on voluntary or chosen celibacy. Was there nothing worth saying about the sanctified sexuality of those whose singleness has *not* been a choice?

You see, celibacy and singleness are not being used as synonyms today. Instead, celibacy is generally considered to be a particular *kind* of singleness—the chosen, intentional, lifelong and purposeful kind. It is also generally seen as a particularly heightened *form* of the unmarried Christian life.

But is a sharp and significant distinction between "chosen celibacy" and "circumstantial singleness" warranted by Scripture? Does the Bible hold out a pre-eminent form of singleness—one that acts as a distinctive vocation or special calling—over and above (or even just significantly distinct from) the situation of all other Christians who are unmarried?

What Do Eunuchs Have to Do with It?

Those who suggest that chosen celibacy is more exceptional than circumstantial singleness often argue their case from the somewhat enigmatic "eunuch passage" of Matthew 19:11-12.

In ancient times, eunuchs were typically men who had either been forcibly castrated (normally before puberty) or born with a physical defect or impediment that rendered them effectively castrated. Because of this, they were generally pitied or even scorned by the pagans of the Roman Empire for not being "real men". For their part, the Jews considered eunuchs to be unclean and cut off from the assembly of God's people (Deuteronomy 23:1). So far, it doesn't sound great for these guys, does it?!

However, there *was* a silver lining to being a eunuch. Because there was no way that they could father children of their own, eunuchs were considered to be pretty safe guys to have hanging around the women of your household. This was especially true if you really, *really* wanted to ensure that your children were actually your children. And so history testifies to a long tradition of eunuchs rising to important positions of authority within powerful households, and especially the royal household. Not only that but they typically served the king (and his family) in the most intimate and private part of his home, the bedchamber. In fact, that is what the Greek word we translate as "eunuch" meant—"bedroom guard". Whether they were eunuchs by birth or by castration, serving the kingdom was their job.

Jesus mentions eunuchs after a discussion with a group of Pharisees about whether a man is allowed to "divorce his wife for any and every reason" (Matthew 19:3). Jesus' answer is, essentially, *no*. The Pharisees consider Jesus' teaching on this topic highly conservative—perhaps even absurdly restrictive (v 4-9). In fact, even his disciples, who have been listening in, are a bit poleaxed! Following his discussion with the religious leaders, they say to him, "If this is the situation between a husband and a wife, it is better not to marry" (v 10). In other words, maybe it is better to just never get married than to risk getting stuck in a "bad" marriage, or divorcing and then not being able to remarry. To this, Jesus replies:

> *Not everyone can accept this word, but only those to whom it has been given. For there are eunuchs who were born that way, and there are eunuchs who have been made eunuchs by others—and there are those who choose to live like eunuchs for the sake of the kingdom of heaven. The one who can accept this should accept it. (v 11-12)*

Those who emphasise the exceptionality of chosen celibacy understand Jesus to be agreeing with his disciples that, in principle, it is better not to marry. However, they point out that Jesus qualifies this when he says, "Not everyone can accept this word [i.e. the disciples' comment that it is better not to marry] ... The one who can accept this should accept it" (v 11-12). What does this mean?

Well, this is where the eunuchs come into it. The first two types of eunuchs (those who are "circumstantially" so) are seen to operate as a kind of counterpoint to the third type of eunuch, which is the real focus (v 12). To put it simply, those who choose to live like a (metaphorical) eunuch for the sake of the kingdom of heaven are those to whom celibacy has been "given" and who can "accept" that it is better for them not to marry.

In this reading, the self-made eunuch is understood to be a metaphor for a select group of Jesus' followers who have been especially called and/or equipped to *choose* lifelong singleness for the sake of the kingdom. As one author puts it, they "have been so seized by the kingdom that all their attention and energy is consumed by it ... Celibacy is a response to an experience of the kingdom, being seized, grasped, swept away by Christ."[14]

That quote gives us insight into the proposed distinction on view between "chosen celibates" and "circumstantial singles". The select few who are "given" to accept lifelong celibacy (like the third type of eunuch) intentionally *choose* it out of love and enthusiasm for the kingdom of God. On the other hand, incidental singles (like the first two types of eunuchs) are not single because of, or for the sake of, the kingdom. Rather their singleness—what some even refer to as "default" or "common" singleness— is simply an unfortunate reality. They aren't "single for Jesus" in the way their intentional and lifelong celibate counterparts are.

Right, so that's the typical reading of Matthew 19:11-12, and certainly the one emphasised by those who promote the exceptionality of chosen or vocational celibacy over circumstantial singleness. But (could you tell that word was coming?), there are some significant, even decisive problems with this interpretation.

When we carefully analyse the original text of these verses, their relationship with Jesus' teaching about divorce and remarriage in the previous verses, and how this passage (and especially the characters of the Pharisees and the disciples) function within Matthew's Gospel as a whole, we arrive at an unexpected, but I think inevitable, conclusion. The self-made eunuch is *not* a metaphor for the disciple who chooses never to marry for the sake of the kingdom, but for the divorced disciple who chooses not to remarry because of their obedience to the kingdom.

Now, I would really love to dive into how the features of this passage lead us towards that conclusion. Sadly, we don't have the space for that here. But never fear! If you are interested in reading a more thorough critique of the "chosen celibacy" reading of Matthew 19 and a fuller outline of the alternative reading I've proposed, I encourage you to take a look at my dedicated four-part online series referenced in this endnote.[15]

In the meantime, here is the relevance of this alternative (and I am convinced, authentic) reading of Matthew 19:11-12 for the sake of this chapter. This is not a passage about choosing lifelong celibacy. Rather, it is a passage about Jesus' teaching on divorce and remaining single after divorce. This means that Jesus is *not* saying that *only* chosen, lifelong singleness counts for the sake of the kingdom. Nor is he saying that a select group of his disciples are specially called and/or equipped for the celibate life. Jesus is not dividing his unmarried disciples into "haves" (chosen celibates) and "have-nots" (circumstantial singles), and then elevating the former over the latter. Chosen celibacy is not of more value to Jesus than circumstantial singleness.

I realise that this brief discussion is unlikely to have persuaded you of the alternative reading of Matthew

19:10-12. (There is so much more to explore on that count, as my four-part series explains!) However, I hope it has at least prompted you to allow that the "obvious" interpretation may not be quite so obvious after all.

Choice and Circumstance—Not a Simple Thing

Pieter is a Christian leader who has proactively committed himself to lifelong singleness. He advocates for others to do the same, in part because, "If singleness is default, and a person can't step any further into it, but a person has to step into marriage to take hold of it, marriage seems more 'filled out'".[16] What Wellum describes as the "unconstrained deliberate choice" of singleness, and Pieter pictures as "stepping into" singleness, is thought to make all the difference to the meaning and significance of one's unmarried status (and so also one's life).

However, if we stop to think about it, it doesn't take long to realise it is simply not true that today's apparently intentional single has stepped into their situation through unconstrained choice. After all, we are all human, and to be human is to be deeply constrained. For one thing, we are constrained by our creatureliness. That is, we are not God. But we are also constrained by our fallenness. That is, we are not good. And so the notion that any of us have unconstrained choice is little more than wishful thinking.

A friend who I'll call Mark has taught me this. He is a wonderfully mature Christian man who experiences unwanted yet persistent and exclusive sexual attraction to other men. He would tell you that he has not actively chosen or cultivated his same-sex attraction. Indeed, he has struggled with it and has prayed that God would take his disordered desires away. Nevertheless, he continues to grapple with them. But Mark is also committed to a biblically faithful understanding of marriage as being between two people of the opposite sex. And so, at this point in his life, he expects to remain unmarried and sexually abstinent.

In other words, Mark has not remained unmarried as a result of his own absolute, unconstrained choice. The circumstances of his life and person have played a significant role in his singleness. Mark has taught me that the single life is as much a result of things that followers of Christ are *not free* to choose as it is a result of things which may indeed be freely chosen.

Similarly, the "circumstantial" single Christian—such as myself—does not truly deserve such a passive moniker. After all, it is not as if I have never exercised any choice or agency in my ongoing singleness. For instance, on more than one occasion I have intentionally said no to a lovely, kind, wonderful single man who has asked me out. I did this because he did not know or love Jesus. Despite my affection for him and my desire to be someone's wife, I made the *active choice* not to take even the first small step away from my singleness because he was not someone in the Lord (see 1 Corinthians 7:39).

Or consider my friend Natalie. Because she would like to be married, many of her friends and family would describe her singleness as "circumstantial". And yet, some years ago, Natalie was on the verge of marriage. She was engaged to a Christian man whom she loved dearly. However, not long before their wedding, Natalie made the agonising decision to end her engagement (and the relationship as a whole) because of a pattern of unrepented habitual sin in her then-fiancé's life. While she has not intentionally chosen to pursue singleness, Natalie *did choose* not to marry that man. She remains single to this day.

All of these examples—along with many others I am sure you can think of from your own life and friendship circles—demonstrate that there is no such thing as pure unconstrained choice or absolute unchosen circumstance in the Christian life. Ultimately, our choices shape our circumstances, and our circumstances shape our choices. But even more significantly than that, it is God who shapes both of these! Proverbs 16:33, which speaks of our circumstances ("The lot is cast into the lap, but its every decision is from the LORD") is complemented by Proverbs 19:21, which speaks of our choices ("Many are the plans in a person's heart, but it is the LORD's purpose that prevails").

Remaining as We Were Called

In 1 Corinthians 7 the apostle Paul offers a flurry of comments directed to different people in different situations: Married people, unmarried people, virgins, widows and widowers, those who are married to non-Christians, those who are betrothed and those who are divorced. But amid all this commotion of marital circumstance and choice, Paul gives a very simple and repeated ethical exhortation that applies to each and every one of them:

> *Nevertheless, each person should live as a believer in whatever situation the Lord has assigned to them, just as God has called them. This is the rule I lay down in all the churches. ... Each person should remain in the situation they were in when God called them. ... Brothers and sisters, each person, as responsible to God, should remain in the situation they were in when God called them.*
>
> *(v 17, 20, 24)*

Put yourself in the shoes of these new Corinthian Christians. The church in your city is only about five years old. You are first-generation baby Christians trying to figure it all out. Many of you were pagans, and your religious and relational life has been turned on its head by the gospel. Your whole sense of self has been completely transformed. And so you find yourself wide-eyed and wondering, "Now we've turned to Christ, what do we need to change about our life situation in order to follow him? What choices do we need to make about our circumstances so we can *really* live for him?"

Paul's response to you is simple: *No changes or new choices are necessary. Simply remain in the situation you were in when God called you to Christ.* He reminds his readers that the God who called them to himself in that situation will—it follows—enable them to live for Jesus in that situation!

Certainly, if the slave can gain their freedom, then they should go for it (v 21). If the betrothed person wants to marry, then they should feel free to do that (v 28, 36). If the widow wants to remarry, then let's plan the wedding (though her would-be husband needs to be "in the Lord", v 39). He says that it is not wrong, let alone sinful, to choose to change one's life situation or to step into something.

However, being a faithful follower of Jesus does not require this of us. Our choices do not make our life situations more meaningful, powerful or fruitful. Indeed, if we bind ourselves to the ideals of a world that stubbornly insists, "It's My Life!" Paul says we are making ourselves slaves all over again! "You were bought with a price," he says, and so "do not become slaves of human beings" (v 23). The grace of God allows you the freedom to remain and serve faithfully in whatever life situation you were in when he called you to himself.

This is truly wonderful news for Kat, Mark, me, and every other unmarried Christian who did not set out to remain single but finds themselves unmarried nonetheless. We are not victims of circumstance. Instead, we are recipients of the singleness assigned to us by the same God who called us to himself. We are not people to whom life has just happened. Instead, we are free to pray for and pursue marriage, even as we submit ourselves to God's will in that. We are not living a less filled out life than our siblings, who have proactively chosen to stay unmarried. Our singleness is not inferior or mediocre. Instead, it has purpose and meaning.

Why? Because in the end, intentionality in singleness is not about the act of intentionally choosing singleness. Rather, it's about intentionally pursuing faithfulness to Christ in our singleness for so long as we *are* single.

It's My Life

Part 2: Living It Out

In his article "Called, not Conscripted (to Celibacy)", Pieter Valk states that those who voluntarily enlist in the armed forces exhibit higher levels of commitment, discipline, productivity and well-being than those who are conscripted. He continues:

> *Oddly enough, the same relationship between forced service versus volunteering for a mission applies to celibacy. Christians who embrace a calling to vocational singleness are more effective and have greater endurance ... Similar to soldiers, when Christians feel forced into celibacy, they may be less willing to sacrifice for the cause of bringing forth Christ's Kingdom ... In contrast, Christians who voluntarily commit to vocational singleness are more effective and have greater endurance for Kingdom work.*[17]

This article (which, unfortunately, provides no evidence to support the comparison above) is one example of an increasing tendency to portray "chosen singles" as intrepid pioneers who bravely set forth into the difficult terrain of faithful Christian singleness. But in truth, our churches have *always* been home to countless unmarried Christians who did not anticipate being single (or becoming single again) but who remain deeply committed to their King and his kingdom within their circumstances.

These men and women are familiar with that difficult terrain. They know many of the potholes and pitfalls. They are eager to come alongside others entering it, to help them find their way. Among their number are many older saints, often sisters in Christ, whose lives testify to an abundance of Spirit-filled faithfulness and fruitfulness... even though it is not the life they expected or chose to step into. These brothers and sisters do not deserve to be sidelined from the story of faithfulness in singleness or have their spiritual fruitfulness diminished. They do not deserve to be made even more invisible simply because their situation is one that they have not sought after or publicly chosen. They *also* deserve our honour, our encouragement and our respect.

In light of that, let me offer some "living it out" suggestions about choice, circumstance and control, first for those who have set out to remain unmarried and then for those who remain open to the possibility of marriage (or perhaps remarriage).

A Word to Those Who Are Single by "Choice"

As we saw in our last chapter, Jesus honours the eunuch (Matthew 19:12). The apostle Paul says it is good for a Christian person to stay unmarried, as he did (1 Corinthians 7:8) and that the betrothed man who is under no compulsion, has control over his desires and has made up his mind not to marry does the right thing (v 37). He even suggests that the widow who chooses not to remarry will be happier if she remains as she is (v 39-40). And so, there is absolutely nothing wrong with seeking to remain single with faithfulness to Christ and his kingdom in mind.

It can take a lot of godly courage and a great deal of hard-fought-for wisdom to make such a decision. It is also a decision that may bring some distinctive challenges. For example, shutting the door on the possibility of loving and being loved as a spouse or parenting children born of your own body can bring immense grief. Some may also have friends and family who are bitterly disappointed in their decision not to marry and who pressure them to change their minds. Of course, choosing to remain single can *also* offer some unique blessings, such as being free to make longer-term plans that don't need to consider the possibility that one day you may marry. If you have set out to remain single with Jesus at the forefront of your mind, know that God's word honours you for that choice, and so do I.

But it is precisely because I honour you that I also want to encourage you to live out your "chosen" singleness with humility. That is the appropriate posture of those who believe that "many are the plans in a person's heart, but it is the LORD's purpose that prevails" (Proverbs 19:21). While God gives us the freedom to make choices and set plans in motion, we should never forget that he remains sovereign over those choices and works all things according to his will. As the psalmist writes, "Our God is in heaven; he does whatever pleases him" (Psalm 115:3). This is why James warns his readers about being overly confident in their plans and decisions:

Now listen, you who say, "Today or tomorrow we will go to this or that city, spend a year there, carry on business

and make money." Why, you do not even know what will
happen tomorrow. What is your life? You are a mist that
appears for a little while and then vanishes. Instead, you
ought to say, "If it is the Lord's will, we will live and do
this or that." (James 4:13-15)

Again, it isn't wrong to make plans to pursue a lifetime
of singleness. But our plans should always be made in
prayerful consideration of, and ongoing submission to, the
Lord's will. In other words, we should be modest planners
and humble choosers.

I know a man—we'll call him Jack—whose intention
it was to remain single for life and who made significant
decisions in light of that intention. However, in his
forties Jack was unexpectedly challenged to consider
becoming a faithful, kind, protective and loving husband
to a Christian woman in vulnerable circumstances. To
cut a long story short, Jack and his wife have now been
married for over a decade. Of course, Jack didn't marry
his wife out of pity! Her circumstances were not the only
factors in play. Among other things, they had developed
a deep mutual affection and an attraction to each other.
But if Jack had been resolutely intent on remaining
single, regardless of the changing context of his and
other people's lives, he would not have been open to the
possibility that God had a different will for him than
his own—and he would have missed out on a wonderful
opportunity to love and serve someone who needed to be
loved and served in this way.

It is for this reason that I want to caution you against
taking any vows of lifelong singleness. As we just saw,
James warns us about the danger of failing to take
God's sovereignty over our lives into account as we make
future plans (James 4:14-15). Jesus also had some very

direct things to say about taking oaths (Matthew 5:33). Faithfulness in marriage requires undertaking and keeping covenantal vows with another person until "death do us part". But faithfulness in singleness requires no such thing. All it demands of you is that you honour God and serve others in your singleness for so long as you are single. Even if you earnestly wish to remain single for the rest of your life, then you can pursue that in God-honouring and other-person-serving ways *without vowing* to remain unmarried come what may. You can publicly demonstrate the goodness of your singleness without performing a novel covenantal ceremony because you feel doing so makes your singleness more legitimate, valuable or real.

You are indeed free to choose to remain single for the sake of the kingdom of heaven. But please make and pursue that choice humbly. And, please, live it out humbly. You are surrounded by a great cloud of other "eunuchs" (both past and present) whose life situation is just as dignified and meaningful as yours, even though it is not one they proactively chose for themselves. Like you, they are getting on with the privilege of living for the sake of the kingdom. Resist any temptation to think of yourself as the one who is *really* willing to live for Jesus' sake.

Yes, your decision may have been—and perhaps still is—painful and difficult for you. But so too can be their daily decision to not put their desire for marriage ahead of God's will for the kind of marriage he would call them to. So, too, can be their daily fight for contentment and belonging in a church that might dismiss their singleness as not as important as, or even inferior to, your own. Let's all seek to learn from and love one another as, together, we serve our King.

A Word to Those Who Are Single by "Circumstance"

I know how bewildering it can be to watch the marriage you so earnestly desire come so naturally to your friends. Indeed, I'm now entering the stage of life where it is starting to come naturally to my friends' children! I know the internal battle that can rage within as you feel simultaneously delighted at but also devastated by another engagement announcement, the delivery of another wedding invitation, or the news of another pregnancy or birth. I know what it can be like to long for something that you just can't make happen for yourself. And I also know what it is to be tempted to make it happen for yourself when you wonder things like "Did God *really say* I shouldn't marry someone who doesn't love Jesus... that godliness in a spouse ought to be a top priority... that remarriage after my divorce is not permissible... that singleness truly is good?"

It is precisely because I know these things myself that I want to urge you to cultivate courage in your "circumstantial" singleness. My brother or sister, we are *not* victims of circumstance. We are not merely single "by default". The author of Proverbs tells us, "The lot is cast into the lap, but its every decision is from the LORD" (Proverbs 16:33). Nothing in this world is purely circumstantial, including your singleness! It has been ordained to you in and for this moment by the one who created your innermost being, who knit you together in your mother's womb, whose eyes saw your unformed body and who wrote all your days in his book before one of them came to be (Psalm 139:13, 16).

You are single because God is sovereign and God is good and God has given you the gift of singleness right here, right now. Remember this: how you feel about your singleness does not determine its dignity or significance in God's sight. And so, it should not determine its dignity or significance in your sight either (or anybody else's). So, let's cultivate the courage to know that the goodness of our singleness is not found in our choosing of it but in the good purposes that God has ordained for it and for us in it.

This courage will involve rejecting the notion that we are "conscripted" to singleness. It will require us to deny the falsehood that, because we haven't intentionally chosen to remain single, we are doomed to be less effective for Jesus in it. And the best way to show such foolishness for what it is is by getting busy serving in our singleness! Of course, I don't mean that we need to be the ones who make sure all the empty spots on the church roster are filled. And, as I hope the last few chapters have shown, I don't mean that the only thing that can make our ongoing singleness good is our instrumental usage of it. Rather, I mean that remaining open to or even actively pursuing marriage is not a reason to be tentative in our service of God, our love of his people and our gospel witness to the watching world.

And while we are on the subject of actively pursuing marriage, let's cultivate the proper courage necessary for that, too. If you desire marriage, then you desire a good thing! It is okay to ask God to give you that good thing and even to seek to change your circumstances in the hope that he might choose to bring it to you. This means that there is nothing inherently wrong with seeking to meet single Christians in the hope that one of them may become your spouse, in trying out online dating to "increase your chances", or in asking trusted friends if they know someone they might introduce you to.

It's perfectly okay, perhaps even good, to actively— though always humbly—do any or all of these things. However, we must have the courage to recognise when too much of a good thing can be bad for us—and, more to the point, bad for our walk with Jesus. Let me explain by way of a personal example.

In my early thirties, I twice signed up for online dating. Both times, I selected a dating platform that was geared towards Christians. I crafted a profile that made it clear I was a committed Christian and that I was only interested in matches who were likewise. I let one or two trusted friends know I had signed up and showed them my profile page. In other words, I was trying to be wise, careful and mature about the whole thing. However, both times, I only lasted a few weeks before I realised I needed to delete my profile and sign out.

Why? Because I had found myself compulsively logging in to check if I had any new matches, if any matches had contacted me, or if any had contacted me back. I frequently revisited profiles, wondering if I had been too hasty in dismissing them, even though I could clearly see that they weren't a mature Christian. I kept reworking my own profile, hoping that minor tweaks might result in more positive outcomes. Essentially, I had become obsessed with the new-found idea of "possibility", and I was thoroughly distracted by how I might turn "possibility" into "reality". Both forays turned the volume of my discontentment up one-thousand-fold. Online dating made it *much, much harder* for me to see my singleness as anything other than something to escape from. And so, after the second time, I decided I needed to be done with it for good.

I'm not saying that all online dating is bad, nor am I suggesting that you would necessarily have the same unhealthy experience as I did. But you might. Or it could be that something else leads you down the same path of increased discontentment and decreased trust in God's goodness (for example, regularly skipping your church to visit others where more singles may be found). We need to have the courage to recognise when attempts to change our circumstances may be making it impossible for us to remain content and, most importantly, trust God in them.

And so, if you long for marriage, then actively pray for it and even pursue it. But be willing to recognise if that pursuit is becoming desperate, if your convictions are becoming compromised or if your yearning for marriage is becoming an unhealthy obsession. In other words, don't allow your desire to be married blind you to the goodness of your singleness. And because it isn't always easy for us to have the objectivity necessary to do that well, it can be wise to ask one or two trusted friends to help you see when your pursuit of a good thing is in danger of becoming not good for you as a disciple of Christ.

Friend, when you are feeling lost or lonely, anxious or afraid, disappointed or despairing as a single Christian who does not want to remain single, courageously ask your good God to help you see the goodness in your singleness—even when, perhaps especially when, you don't *want* to see it as good. And always remember, our God is both loving and powerful. Your circumstances are not outside his control, nor are they counter to his promise to do good for and through you.

Be Thou My Vision

Part 1: Being Distracted
Versus Being Devoted

My social-media feeds often feature photos of my married friends out at a fancy restaurant for their wedding anniversary, or a less fancy restaurant on a more regular date night, or enjoying a beachside vacation with their kids over summer. I love seeing photos of my friends enjoying married and family life. But when I post similar photos of me enjoying my single life, I can't help but feel that some who see them are quietly thinking, "Dani certainly seems to be living it up, doesn't she? Must be nice..."

Mel feels the same way. "It's like I'm not meant to enjoy any of the freedom or fun that can be part and parcel of my singleness," she told me. "In fact, I feel like I'm *not allowed* to enjoy it—because, if I do, it means I'm being self-indulgent." Mel is far from alone. So many Christian singles feel that if their singleness is to be truly acceptable, it must also be austere. Certainly, they are allowed to enjoy *parts* of life. But when that enjoyment arises directly out of their singleness, well, that's when the pursed lips and side glances can start being directed their way.

Where has this thinking come from? It all goes back to that good old chapter of 1 Corinthians 7, or rather, to our usual interpretation of one particular part of the chapter (in bold below):

> [29] *What I mean, brothers and sisters, is that the time is short. From now on those who have wives should live as if they do not;* [30] *those who mourn, as if they did not; those who are happy, as if they were not; those who buy something, as if it were not theirs to keep;* [31] *those who use the things of the world, as if not engrossed in them. For this world in its present form is passing away.* [32] ***I would like you to be free from concern. An unmarried man is concerned about the Lord's affairs—how he can please the Lord.*** [33] ***But a married man is concerned about the affairs of this world—how he can please his wife—*** [34] ***and his interests are divided. An unmarried woman or virgin is concerned about the Lord's affairs: her aim is to be devoted to the Lord in both body and spirit. But a married woman is concerned about the affairs of this world—how she can please her husband.*** [35] *I am saying this for your own good, not to restrict you, but that you may live in a right way in undivided devotion to the Lord. (v 29-35)*

Here's how we usually understand Paul's logic in these verses: singleness is a good thing, *but*, only so long as the single person isn't distracted from putting it to good use, is entirely undivided in their devotion to the Lord, and is not thinking about themselves in any way. If not, then singleness is often considered to be compromised, illegitimate and perhaps even rebellious.

A married person gets a hall-pass on being divided in their devotion (something we'll come back to a bit later).

But singles don't. And so, this passage is frequently translated into an expectation of instrumental austerity in singleness. But once again, if we take another look at the passage, we discover that our usual interpretation and application of it may have a few problems. In this chapter, I want to unpick some of the issues and suggest what I believe to be a better reading instead.

The Complexity of Being Single

One author has described the instrumental value of singleness this way: it means the single person is "able to say 'yes' to things that require more of you than a married person can afford".[18] This was recently put in practical terms by someone who shared with me how certain of their single friends felt 1 Corinthians 7:32-34 was being "weaponised" against them in a particular ministry context. As he put it, they were told they "were 'free' from other concerns and therefore should work longer and harder with less time off" than their married colleagues. Even if we're not in paid ministry, unmarried Christians are very used to being told they are obliged to do more, give more, spend more, sacrifice more, *be more* than their married counterparts.

Perhaps single Christians think about this obligation as they head home after a long day at work—but only after they've stopped at the grocery store to grab the ingredients (for the dinner they are solely responsible for preparing, as usual) which they didn't have time to buy on the weekend because they had to run all the household errands alone. They think about it as they wonder, yet again, how they will manage to pay all this month's bills from their solo income. They think about it when they get a message from their parents asking them to make themselves available for a family visit this coming weekend because their brother and his family's plans have now changed, and the unstated rules say that the single one always has to readjust their schedule around everyone else...

Okay, I'm being slightly snarky, but you get my point. Married people are not the only ones for whom life is complex. Whether it is the exhaustion of not having someone to shoulder day-to-day life with, juggling the uncertainty of housing options as a single person, bearing the financial burden of a lifetime spent paying up to one million dollars more in taxes and healthcare than those who are married (in the USA at least),[19] or any number of other stressors, singles don't live a magically untroubled life of endless freedom, flexibility and opportunity. And so an overly simplistic read of 1 Corinthians 7:29-35 doesn't make practical (or loving) sense of the daily existence of most single Christians today.

On (Not) Being Worldly

But an oversimplistic reading of those verses also fails to make *biblical sense.*

Consider Paul's comments about how a married Christian is concerned about the "affairs of this world" (v 33, 34), while the unmarried Christian is concerned about "the Lord's affairs" (v 32, 34). A customary reading of this passage suggests that although a single person needs to be entirely devoted to the concerns of the Lord, a married person is primarily responsible for being concerned about their spouse. But notice how Paul describes these concerns of the married person: they are concerns about "the affairs of this world". And, well, the world and its affairs don't exactly get a good rap from Paul, or indeed any other biblical author.

1 Corinthians repeatedly speaks of the world as that which stands opposed to God. "The world ... did not know"

God (1:21), and its wisdom is subverted by the message of the cross (v 20-29). Believers are to watch out lest they "be finally condemned with the world" (11:32; see also 2:12; 3:19; 6:2). Commentators Brian Rosner and Roy Ciampa put it like this: the letter of 1 Corinthians "is a timeless challenge to Christians of all generations and in all places not to be conformed to the world".[20]

This idea is not confined to 1 Corinthians. Paul frequently writes of this world's darkness, sinfulness, and enslavement (e.g. Galatians 4:3; Colossians 2:8) and rejoices that Christians no longer follow the ways of the world (e.g. Ephesians 2:2). Likewise, James says that "friendship with the world means enmity towards God" (James 4:4), while Peter rejoices that those who know Jesus have "escaped the corruption in the world" (2 Peter 1:4; 2:20). The apostle John exhorts his readers to "not love the world or anything in the world" (1 John 2:15), and Jesus himself teaches his disciples that they "are not of the world, just as I am not of it" (John 17:16).

Over and over again, Scripture is clear. Christians no longer belong to the world and its affairs, but to their Lord and *his* affairs. And so, why in the world (pun intended) would these three verses in 1 Corinthians 7 break ranks and *actively commend* married Christians for being concerned about the affairs of the world?

Perhaps Paul meant that marriage is worldly only in the sense that, like this world, it is temporary (v 31)— something we have already seen is indeed true. But even so, because the world's "passing away" is directly connected to the fact that it is fallen (see Romans 8:20-22), Paul instructs the Corinthian Christians to be people "who deal with the world as though they had no dealings with it" (1 Corinthians 7:31, ESV). So why, in the very next verses, would he be actively commending married Christians for being anxious about certain concerns of the world, and especially when he makes a direct comparison between those and the concerns of the Lord?

This is our first clue that there is something more—perhaps even something quite different—going on in these verses than we usually think today.

Divided or Devoted?

Take another look at verses 32-34. Notice how the corresponding comparisons of being divided or devoted are mixed in with the contrast of either being concerned with the affairs of this world or of the Lord. Again, we usually understand Paul as saying it is right, or at least understandable, that married Christians will have divided interests. But is Scripture *really* saying that it is okay for husbands and wives to be divided in their personal devotion to God?

The apostle Paul didn't seem to think so. After all, in the very next verse, he explains that the purpose behind his exhortations in verses 32-34 is so that his readers "may live in a right way in undivided devotion to the Lord" (v 35). It could be that Paul particularly had his unmarried readers in mind as he wrote those words (that is, he was giving them a good reason not to marry). But does that mean he was content for his married readers to *not* live in the same right way of undivided devotion to the Lord? Does he think that marriage makes this an outright impossibility?

I find that very difficult to wrap my head around, especially because what Paul says in verse 35 echoes what we read elsewhere in Scripture, not least from Jesus himself: "Love the Lord your God with all your heart and with all your soul and with all your mind. This is the greatest and first commandment" (Matthew 22:37).

Loving God with *all* of us is repeated three times for emphasis. The second greatest commandment—to love others—flows out of this first and primary one. Given this, why would Paul say a married Christian *can't* and *shouldn't* aim for the same kind of undivided devotion to God as the single Christian? Is a spouse the Lord's competitive rival for a married Christian's love and attention?

In Colossians 3, Paul writes, "Whatever you do, whether in word or deed, do it all in the name of the Lord Jesus" (v 17). He then *immediately* says what it means for husbands, wives, parents and children (and slaves and masters) to love each other. He concludes that, as they love each other in word and deed, "it is the Lord Christ you are serving" (v 24). In other words, the marriage relationship is not a distraction from service to the Lord. It *is* a way to serve him! We'll return to this in our next "Living It Out" discussion.

If we read 1 Corinthians 7:32-24 as saying the single Christian is to be totally devoted to God, while the married Christian is right to be divided in their devotion to him, I fear we misread the passage in its immediate and broader biblical context. Surely, whether we are married or single, Jesus' sacrificial devotion to us—so all-in that it saw him nailed to the cross—can only be rightly met by nothing less than our full and undivided devotion to him.

My friend Rebecca recently gave me a glimpse of precisely this as she reflected on the wedding of a couple from her church. She said, "Of many highlights, my top one was probably watching them sing, 'Thou and thou only the first in my heart' while looking at each other and knowing they both knew they weren't singing about each other". Regardless of whether we are married or single, it is *the Lord* who is to "Be Thou My Vision", the first in our heart.

When Pleasing Is Not Pleasing

Here's where we've got to so far: we are right to recognise that in verses 32-34, Paul *does* say divided devotions exist for married Christians. However, I have suggested that we're wrong to assume that he is saying that those divided devotions are a good or even simply an acceptable thing. To put it another way, Paul does not commend married Christians for being concerned with pleasing their spouse at the expense of, or instead of, pleasing the Lord.

Now, that last sentence doesn't mean Christian spouses shouldn't care deeply about or prioritise each other. Of course they should! However, we need to interrogate this language of "pleasing" a little.

Notably, none of the New Testament passages that speak about how Christian husbands and wives should relate to, love and serve one another (e.g. Ephesians 5:22-31; Colossians 3:18-19; 1 Peter 3:1-7) encourages them to "please" each other. This means there is no reason for us to automatically assume the verb "please" in 1 Corinthians 7:32-24 is synonymous with the appropriate love and care that Scriptures calls spouses to offer one another… and especially not when it involves pleasing them over pleasing God.

It's not that the act of "pleasing" must always be a bad thing. Paul goes on to say that he seeks to "please everyone in every way", with the hope "that they may be saved" (10:33). But when it comes down to a choice between pleasing God or pleasing other humans, the choice ought to be an obvious one. As Paul explains in 1 Thessalonians 2:4, God's people should not be interested in "trying to please people but God, who tests our hearts".

So then, in the context of this passage, "pleasing" one's spouse is not necessarily the same thing as loving them faithfully, serving them well, or rightly prioritising their interests (e.g. forgoing a particular ministry opportunity because it would mean neglecting them). Rather, it is connected with being anxious and concerned about your husband or wife from a worldly and divided perspective.

This is hard for us to get our heads around because often Christians are taught that marriage is *the place* in which God does his best sanctifying work. Ironically, we might think that it is single Christians who most struggle with having a worldly and divided perspective! We might also have been encouraged to think it is impossible to prioritise a spouse's interests too much. Yet here, in 1 Corinthians 7, Paul claims that marriage brings "worldly [literally, fleshly] troubles" (v 28, ESV). He says that being a husband or wife can make it *harder* to be fully devoted to God, and that there exists a chronic temptation for married people to "please" their spouse in a worldly rather than a God-honouring way.

What does that look like in practice? Perhaps the adage of "happy wife = happy life" may tempt a husband to prioritise keeping his wife "happy" rather than seeking to love her in ways that are, occasionally, more difficult and demanding for both of them. Perhaps a wife might idealise her husband such that she begins to see only him, relying on her husband for what she ought to instead turn to God for. Or perhaps, as a married friend of mine suggested, "worldliness means married people can look for 'not being alone' in the wrong place", leading to a marriage that is unhealthily co-dependent and relationally isolated.

There are any number of ways in which a tendency towards "pleasing" one's spouse may evidence a preoccupation with worldly things and a divided heart.

How to Secure Undivided Devotion
Paul doesn't want his readers to get caught up in these

worldly anxieties and divided distractions. But how are they to avoid doing so? The answer is in the previous verses:

> *But if you do marry, you have not sinned; and if a virgin marries, she has not sinned. But those who marry will face many troubles in this life [literally, tribulation in the flesh], and I want to spare you this. What I mean, brothers and sisters, is that the time is short. From now on those who have wives should live as if they do not; those who mourn, as if they did not; those who are happy, as if they were not; those who buy something, as if it were not theirs to keep; those who use the things of the world, as if not engrossed in them. For this world in its present form is passing away. (v 28-31)*

One way to be spared the "fleshly tribulations" and worldly dividedness that marriage fosters is not to get married at all. And we certainly see Paul encouraging that throughout 1 Corinthians 7!

But in this passage, Paul also presents an alternative option. He says a Christian person *can* get married while not allowing themselves to become engrossed in and entrapped by the affairs of this temporary world that our enemy wants to draw them into. That is, they can be married while *still* pursuing undivided devotion to the Lord. How?

The Early Church Father John Chrysostom had the same question. He asked, "How can marriage be honorable, which so hinders us?" But then he immediately provided his own answer: "It is possible, yea very possible, even if we have wives, to pursue after virtue, if we will. How? If having 'wives', we 'be as though we had none'."[21] It's a quote from Paul in verse 29: "From now on *those who have wives should live as if they do not*".

Married, but as If Not Married?!

What an odd thing to say! What on earth does Paul mean by that? Well, because of what he has already said in 1 Corinthians 7, we know what he *can't* mean: namely, that Christians should never marry, should stop being married or should stop having sex with each other. But if Paul isn't saying any of those things, what then *is* he saying? The Early Church Father, Augustine, helps us to understand. He quotes verses 32-33 and says that in those very verses...

> *to some extent [Paul] **explains what he had already said** [in verse 29]: "Let them that have wives be as though they had none." For they who have wives in such a way as to care for the things of the Lord, how they may please the Lord, without having any care for the things of the world in order to please their wives, are, in fact, just as if they had no wives.*[22]

According to Augustine, Paul is not giving married Christians a hall-pass on being divided in their devotion to God. No, he instead shows that the married person who lives as if they do not have a husband or a wife (v 29) is the married person who lives like the unmarried person celebrated in verses 32 and 34!

The godly single Christian is Paul's aspirational model of someone who is *not* caught up in the fleshly tribulations of marriage, not divided in their devotion between the Lord and a spouse, and not preoccupied with this type of the world's affairs over the Lord's affairs. He encourages Christians who have a spouse to live as if they do not by following the example of their single counterparts in this specific sense. Because he wants them to be undivided and undistracted *in their marriages,* Paul is telling his married readers to learn from—indeed to be like—his unmarried readers!

Hopelessly Devoted to You

At the beginning of this chapter, I cited an author who argues that the single Christian is "able to say 'yes' to things that require more of [them] than a married person can afford".[23] But I think this misunderstands Paul's meaning in 1 Corinthians 7:32-35.

Paul calls his married readers not to be engrossed in the concerns that, in a fallen world, married people can easily become entangled in. And so he urges them to look to the example of the godly unmarried Christian to understand what that kind of devoted life looks like. After all, what better example is there of someone living as if they do not have a spouse than the one who literally does not have a spouse!

Now, of course, this understanding has a whole lot of implications not only for married Christians but also for those of us who are unmarried. And we will explore those implications next. But to whet your appetite, let me share with you some words sent to me by Judith, a lifelong single woman and former cross-cultural missionary:

> For me, this passage is not about the time available for ministry. Not having a husband means I do not wrestle with the kind of divided heart and mind that Paul says my married friends do. Jesus gets my undivided (though yes, imperfect) loyalty. Oh, how wonderful to walk with Jesus first!

Be Thou My Vision

Part 2: Living It Out

Perhaps your mind is still reeling a little bit from the last chapter. We covered some dense stuff! And I imagine you are wondering what this all *actually* means in practice. Well, let's unpack that, first for those of us who are single and then for those who are married (or who may get married).

Undivided Devotion in Singleness

For so long as you do not have a husband or a wife, you are a living, breathing, walking, talking example of what it is to live life spared from the many troubles which Paul says married people face in this life (1 Corinthians 7:28). *This* is what it means that you are undivided in your devotion to the Lord, and what Paul calls married Christians to emulate by looking to you.

This means that your married brothers and sisters *need* you. They need you to be models of devotion. They need to learn about being undivided from you. They need to witness how you are deeply concerned with the Lord's affairs and to model what it looks like to live as one not engrossed in a (good) relationship that will eventually pass away. As my friend Brooke explains, "I don't know exactly what my married friends' lives are like, but as someone whose singleness means I am free to be concerned about the Lord's affairs, I get to ask about and listen to their experience of marital life from a place of curiosity. I can offer insights that don't stem from personal experience but are grounded in Scripture and which are offered out of love for them and concern for their spiritual maturity."

All of this means that those of us who are single need to be models of devotion worth looking to. We need to be able to demonstrate to others what this kind of being undivided means in practice. We need to be deeply concerned with the Lord's affairs and be able to model what it is not to be engrossed in this aspect of our world, whose present form of passing away. This is our privilege before God. But it is also our responsibility to him and to others.

Now, at this point, you may be thinking, "Here we go again with the whole 'singles have more time, energy, and money to do more God-stuff than married Christians do'". So, let's take a moment to be honest about that. You and I both know that there *are* various times and seasons of the single life when many of us *do* have more of these things. And so, when that *is* the case, we should proactively express our undivided devotion through the "more" that God has given us. Serving the Lord is not a burden—it's a joy. If we somehow resent the opportunity to do more for the one who gave all for us, then something has gone wrong in our thinking... and in our hearts. We've become divided.

And yet, we also know it is simply not true that singles always have significantly more flexibility, energy and resources than our married counterparts. We still have busy, complicated, work-filled, errand-bound, time-poor, financially-challenged, relationally-complex lives that are often made more so by the fact that we are doing most, if not all, of these things alone. We don't always have more time or more anything. This is especially true if we are a single parent.

But here's the thing I really want you to understand: *1 Corinthians 7:29-35 is not ultimately about you having more (or less) time, energy or resources.* The outworking of this passage is not that singles ought to be plugging every gap on their church rosters, signing up for every mission trip going, always running the children's ministry at church and having no rest, relaxation or fun in their life.

Remember, our unique advantage is that we are spared the "worldly troubles" of marriage (v 28, ESV). We don't need to constantly fight the gravitational pull that sees us tempted to pragmatically "please" a spouse (as opposed to loving and serving them as Scripture exhorts). We don't need to resist the gravitational pull of being consumed with one (very important) relationship over and above all else, and especially over and above our relationship with the Lord. And so this passage is not about us having *more* of one thing (time, energy or money) but about us having *less*—indeed, a total absence—of something else (the particular troubles and tribulations of marriage).

Contrary to all of the books, articles and sermons that insist that marriage is the fast track to sanctification and the express lane to holiness, 1 Corinthians 7:29-35 says that marriage makes it *more difficult* to live in undivided devotion to the Lord! This means we singles need to recognise that as good as marriage is, it is not a "silver bullet" that will make our Christian life perfect, whole, easier or less complicated. In fact, Paul suggests it will do just the opposite... and he wants to spare us that (v 28). We need to hear God's word: if we do marry, our new situation *will* bring fleshly tribulation. It *will* tempt us away from undivided devotion to the Lord. It is very important we recognise the privilege we have in being spared all of that. It is just as important for us to discern the significance of what it would mean to lose that privilege by getting married.

But even if we do still wish to actively pursue marriage (and again, we are free to do that!) we should actively prepare ourselves to *not* be entrapped in the division and distraction that *will* come if we do marry. How do we do that here and now? Remember, it is not primarily about the time we have to be devoted but the character of our devotion. And so, it will mean focusing on things like growing to know and love God's word, dedicating ourselves to prayer, cultivating the spiritual fruits he is bearing in us, not neglecting to meet with his people, investing deeply in a breadth of relationships and so on. But it will also mean not allowing our present undistracted devotion to be utterly hijacked by our efforts to "escape" our singleness. My single friend, don't become so consumed by the prospect of finding a spouse that you fail to capitalise on the particular spiritual blessings that are yours while you don't have one.

But, wait. Have I just brought us right back onto the instrumental loop? Am I saying that the value and significance of being single is only found in the fact that we can "usefully" use our singleness by being totally devoted to the Lord?

Well, yes. But also no. Singles *are* called to be undivided in their devotion to God. But this is not a distinctive call for singles alone. Rather, it is for each and every Christian person. Paul wants *all* of us to live in a right way before the Lord (v 35). Whether single or married, male or female, young or old, in plenty or in want, the aim of the Christian life is to look to our Saviour and say "Be Thou

My Vision". As Paul exhorts his readers later in the same letter, "Whatever you do, do it all for the glory of God" (1 Corinthians 10:31).

This brings us to a final application of this passage for us singles. Where the first raised the bar on the unmarried life of devotion, this second one testifies to the freedom we have to enjoy that life of devotion.

Undivided devotion is not about spending every moment of our day in austere service. Instead, it is about loving God with all our heart, soul, strength and mind. It's about doing everything for his glory. And so, it is okay to delight in the single life that the God we glorify has given us. We can embrace the things we enjoy about being single without feeling guilty for enjoying ourselves. We are free to have fun in our singleness because experiencing enjoyment, pleasure, satisfaction and contentment is, quite wonderfully, part of God's good creative intention for human life. This means we can bring glory to him *by* delighting in the glorious things he has graciously given us!

Yes, we must be careful not to become self-focused and self-indulgent. While the married person too easily becomes concerned about the world's affairs (pleasing their spouse), we singles can too easily become concerned about *our own affairs* (pleasing ourselves). And so, we must be on our guard against that by devoting ourselves to the Lord's affairs (pleasing him). But we can absolutely do that while still enjoying the parts of our singleness that bring us godly delight, satisfaction and fun. So, single friend, go have fun on vacation for the glory of God!

Undivided Devotion in Marriage

In case you skipped over the section directed to singles, let me repeat something I said in it. Contrary to all of the books, articles and sermons that insist marriage is the fast track to sanctification, 1 Corinthians 7:29-35 actually says that marriage makes it *more* difficult to live in undivided devotion to the Lord. That may be a bit discomforting for you, a married Christian, to read. But please hear me when I say that it doesn't mean that your marriage is somehow bad or worse than singleness. It doesn't mean that you should not have got married. It doesn't mean that you aren't able to live as those concerned about the Lord's affairs.

However, it *does* mean that you need to reckon with the difficult dual truths that first, your marriage *will* bring you particular trouble in this world that, in turn, will threaten to generate division in your wholehearted devotion to the Lord, and second, that God does not want you to be divided in this way. And so, hear the words of C.S. Lewis:

> When I have learnt to love God better than my earthly dearest, I shall love my earthly dearest better than I do now. In so far as I learn to love my earthly dearest at the expense of God and instead of God, I shall be moving towards the state in which I shall not love my earthly dearest at all. When first things are put first, second things are not suppressed but increased.[24]

In other words, your spouse and your Saviour are not in competition for your attention and loyalty. Instead, your devotion, love and concern for your spouse (and so too any children you may have) should flow directly out of your primary devotion, love and concern for your Saviour. When that's the case, you will not be engrossed by your spouse (or your children), nor your relationship with them, at the expense of loving Jesus.

Now, I can't tell you precisely what that ought to look like for you in your marriage, but I can share glimpses of how I've seen it expressed in the marriages of certain friends of mine. It is abundantly clear to me that these men and women love each other deeply. Yet I'm not only talking lovey-dovey romantic love, but also deep, abiding and sometimes difficult love. They apply themselves to fulfilling the promises they made to each other on their wedding day. This includes repenting and seeking forgiveness from the other when they fail to love patiently or perfectly. They are committed to their own faithfulness and to each other's godliness within their marriages.

And yet, while they rightly prioritise each other's needs and spiritual maturity, they do not make "pleasing" each other their main game—and certainly not at the expense of pleasing their Lord. They sincerely want each other to be happy, and they work towards that, but they don't regard each other's happiness as the key performance indicator of their marriage. They model to me (and many others) how their love for each other flows out of their foundational love for their God. But they also show me how that same foundational love of God flows out into love for others—whether that be family, friends or strangers. While they adore each other, they are not so absorbed with each other that they exclude or diminish everyone else.

Put simply, they do not seek to balance an equation of how much time, energy and resources they have to devote to the Lord versus each other versus other people. Rather, they focus on the *character* of their devotion to him, which is then lived out in loving relationships with God, their spouse, and other people.

If you are married, then the task God's word has set you is not always an easy or straightforward one. And yet, neither you nor your spouse can afford to be so caught up in the things of this world (and each other) that you are divided in your devotion to your Lord and Saviour. And so, let me urge you to look to godly single Christians for examples of what undivided and undistracted devotion can look like.

Perhaps you are already doing this, in which case, keep going! (And as a side note, make sure your single friends know that they are serving you in this way. They'll be deeply encouraged to hear it!) Or perhaps this is something you could apply yourself to more diligently. In which case, let me suggest that a place to start is by making sure you see, know and spend time with single members of your church. After all, it's hard to emulate someone whose life you don't see up close and personal.

Friend, the time is now short. The present form of this world is passing away. Whether married or single, those of us who belong to Christ are to live as those who are not engrossed with this world and its affairs. We are to be dedicated to undivided devotion to him. He is to be our vision, the Lord of our hearts.

6

Let's Talk About Sex

Part 1: Both More and
Less Than You Think

The first concert I ever attended without a parental chaperone was Salt-N-Pepa—the all-female hip-hop trio of '90s fame. (Yes, I'm aware that ages me. A lot!) One of Salt-N-Pepa's most famous songs was "Let's Talk About Sex". Google tells me that it only made it to No. 13 on the US charts, but it hit No. 1 in my home country of Australia.

While Salt-N-Pepa may have got us all talking about sex back in 1991, it feels as if we haven't stopped talking about it since. But all this talking about sex can be a real challenge for Christians who are single. The way and extent to which we tend to talk about sex today—even in the church—so often leaves chaste single Christians feeling that they are missing out on the best that life has to offer. Actually, it is more than that. It can leave them feeling as if they are missing out on being fully human.

Christian author Stephen McAlpine calls our day in the 21st-century West the "Sexular Age".[25] He's on to something: our culture is not only deeply secularised but also profoundly sexualised. Our individual sexual appetites, instincts, desires and wants are not simply considered foundational to what it means to be a human being but to what it means for each of us to be the individual human person that we *uniquely are*. Throughout most of history, sex was an activity humans did for the sake of procreation, pleasure and partnership. But now, sex lies at the heart of who the world says we are; to not be having sex with whom we choose is to be less than fully ourselves.

Unfortunately, it is not only the world that has put sex at the very heart of human identity. We Christians have actively helped co-author the Sexular Age in which we now live. It is for this reason that we need to reckon with the part *the church* itself has played in our society's obsession with sex.

Reforming Sex

Our story starts back in 16th-century Europe at the time of the Protestant Reformation, when key Christians began to "protest" against certain teaching and corresponding corruption within the Roman Catholic Church of the time. It is difficult to overstate the significance of the Reformation on all manner of subjects. But included in that list is the Reformers' thinking on sex, marriage and singleness, which would go on to have a profound impact, not only on the newly formed Protestant church but on the Western world for centuries to come.

In order to understand how and why this was the case, we first need to explore the historical place of celibacy—by which I mean here, consecrated vows of lifelong singleness and sexual abstinence.

Celibacy was a widespread practice throughout medieval Europe and had become compulsory for priests around AD 1130. During the High Middle Ages (1000–1300), monasteries and nunneries were brimming with those who had undertaken vows of poverty, obedience and chastity. And by the middle of the millennium, the celibate life had come to be seen as a set-apart and elevated vocation. Monks and nuns were depicted as heroically holy figures, while celibate priests were thought to be the necessary mediators between God and all the common (married) folk. But there was a dark side to all this celibacy: sexual immorality was fairly pervasive among the celibate ranks. Illegitimate children had the run of the monasteries, and mistresses were housed in priests' residences.

Key Reformers were rightly appalled by the hypocrisy of those who set themselves up on the celibate pedestal, all while committing secret (or not-so-secret) sexual sin. But they were also outraged at the way that being celibate was said to make you holier and draw you closer to God and salvation. And so, the protesting Reformers actively opposed the Roman Catholic Church's teaching that a priest, monk or nun could essentially earn themselves brownie points with God through their celibacy. They also wanted to rehabilitate the goodness of marriage among Christian commoners and leaders alike.

The writings and teachings of the 16th-century German Reformer Martin Luther were particularly important on this topic. As a young man, Luther had become a celibate monk. However, he later came to (strongly!) believe that the church was mandating celibacy in a way that the Bible didn't. And so, Luther embarked on a long-term effort to renew the church's vision for marriage as a good, natural and godly vocation in the Christian life. Part of the way in which he did that was by claiming that the church had made far too much of celibacy.

While Luther could admit that faithful singleness was theoretically good, he saw it as unattainable for the vast majority of Christians. Why? Well, because he understood that God's mandate for humans to be fruitful and multiply (Genesis 1:28) meant that humans *needed* to have sex.

> *Therefore, just as God does not command anyone to be a man or a woman but creates them the way they have to be, so he does not command them to multiply but creates them so that **they have to multiply**. And wherever men try to resist this, it remains irresistible nonetheless and goes its way through fornication, adultery, and secret sins, for this is a matter of nature and not of choice.*[26]

In other words, Luther thought that humanity's very created nature compels us to have sex. In fact, he spoke of sex as being "more necessary than sleeping and waking, eating and drinking, and emptying the bowels and the bladder"![27] If humanity needs to have sex as much as, if not more than, they need to go to the toilet, then the logical conclusion is that every Christian needs to marry (or else fall into endless sexual sin). In fact, according to Luther, the only people who didn't need to marry for the sake of their holiness were those in whom "God performs a miracle by means of a special gift".[28] To his mind, such people were no more than one in one thousand. Others, such as the French Reformer John Calvin, also taught that the only people who could resist their drive towards sex were those who had "a special gift which God has withheld from many".[29]

Yes, *this* is the moment that the (so-called) "gift of singleness" as a spiritual empowerment bursts onto the scene. It was the Protestant Reformers who popularised—dare we say, invented—the notion that an unmarried Christian could only live a godly life of sexual faithfulness so long as God had given them a super-duper special gift to do so.

An Inherited Overcorrection

The Reformation was an extraordinarily important time of renewal within the church. We have so very much to be thankful to the Reformers for. And yet, I fear that their teaching on sex (and so also on marriage and singleness) is not one of those things—or at least, not in full. Yes, the Reformers rightly sought to correct corrupted institutional celibacy and rediscover marriage as a good part of this creation. But in trying to make more of "mundane" marriage and less of "heroic" celibacy, the Reformers ended up making far too much of sex. They overcorrected. And we have inherited that legacy.

This is why, as the world has increasingly placed our sexual desires more and more at the heart of what it means for us to be who we really are, Protestant Christians have been quietly nodding along. After all, we have a Reformed tradition that insists that we have been *created to have sex*—a tradition that puts having sex at the very heart of what it means to be a human person. In this sense, this Protestant theology of sex has linked hands with a worldly ideology of sex. The end result has been that both the world *and* large parts of the church now tend to see sex not simply as something we do but as part of who we are.

We have made sex into far too big a thing. And yet, the tragic irony is that, in doing this, we have also made sex into far too small a thing.

Lessons from the Future

In our first chapter, we considered Jesus' teaching that resurrected human beings will not be married to each other (Matthew 22:29-30). Instead, we will be "single" sons and daughters of God, unmarried brothers and sisters in Christ. But note something important about my choice of words in those last two phrases. We will be *brothers* and *sisters*. We will be *sons* and *daughters*. This is because I want to argue that, in the new creation, we will still be human men and women.

Our having been created as either male or female is a foundational part of our humanity. And so, our sexual nature isn't something that can just be done away with in the resurrection age. If it was, then we wouldn't be *new* creations but entirely *different* creations. Just as Jesus was recognisably himself (after the resurrection), and so, by implication, recognisably male, so I have every expectation that when you and I meet in eternity (and I hope we will!) you will be meeting the perfected, transformed, embodied, *female person* named Dani.

And yet, as we have already established in a previous chapter, you'll be meeting a perfected woman who will not be having sex (nor, for that matter, giving birth to babies). My female sexed nature will remain central to who I am in eternity. But it will not be expressed or experienced through the act of, or desire for, sexual intercourse itself. This means that looking at our sexual personhood from the perspective of eternity teaches us something far fuller, bigger, and better than anything the "Sexular" world has to offer.

First, eternity teaches us that sexual intercourse is not the ultimate reason behind God's creation of us as sexed males and females. According to Jesus, the wonderful earthly expression of our sexual nature through sexual intercourse in marriage won't carry over into eternity where we will be "single" ever after (Matthew 22:29-30). And yet, it seems that we *will still* retain our sexually distinct natures as men and women. That is, while sex won't continue to exist, our sexual selves will. And if that is so, it follows that God's creation of us as either male or female is ultimately about much more than simply what we do between the sheets in this creation. Eternity teaches us that our sexual natures are purposed for something greater and more enduring than earthly sex alone.

Which of course leads us to ask, what exactly is this greater and more enduring purpose behind our sexual personhood? Well, hold that thought because we'll return to it in a little bit. For the moment, our lesson is a simple one: even if single Christians never, ever have sex, eternity testifies to the fact that their sexual natures are *still deeply meaningful* in ways we will soon explore. Indeed, we might say that faithfully celibate singles are living the sexed life of eternity in the here and now.

Following on from this, eternity teaches us that our sense of self is not ultimately determined by who we want to have sex with and the kind of sex we want to have with them. Our "Sexular" world insists that a person's sexual inclinations, longings and attractions reveal who they are deep down. It says that we need to be free to embrace and act on our sexual desires if we wish to become our true and authentic selves. As a result, chaste single Christians are either pitied as those who are living a life of miserable self-suppression or valorised as martyrs who make the greatest form of self-sacrifice imaginable.

But eternity has something different to say to us. In the new creation we will be the most fulfilled and perfect human people it is possible for us to be. Our resurrected bodies will be glorified, imperishable, powerful, splendorous and immortal (1 Corinthians 15:35-58; Philippians 3:21). Not only that, but we will finally be people who fully know and are fully known (1 Corinthians 13:10-12). There, we will be the very best a man (or woman) can get! And yet, we will not have sex nor, it follows, desire to have sex.

This means that the world (and, too often, the church) is wrong. When you are your very best self, sexual desire for intercourse won't even be in the mix. And so your sexual desires and attractions cannot be determinative or definitive of your ultimate sense of personal identity—of who you are at the most authentic level.

This is why I choose to use the terms "sexual nature" and "sexuality" interchangeably. The world around us typically understands our "sexuality" to refer to our attractional patterns and desires. But eternity teaches us that our true sexuality is not merely a matter of who we are sexually attracted to and how we then behave as a result. Our creaturely sexuality must be about much more than just those things that are for this earth only.

So, if our sexuality is about more than just our desires, then *what is it* about? Well, again, hold your horses. We are getting there! For the moment, my point is this: the sexually chaste single Christian is not a victim whose truest self is being suppressed. Neither is sexual abstinence in singleness an immense sacrifice that entails denying who we are at our very core. In fact, chaste single Christians show the rest of us how foolish it is to reduce the core of our sexuality down to merely what we want to do with our genitals and who we want to do those things with.

Finally, eternity teaches us that being a female or male person is not ultimately defined by the earthly vocations connected to sexual intercourse—namely, being a spouse or a parent. Marriage and parenthood are very good and important aspects of our earthly human existence. This means that we are not free to redefine what it is to be male or female in ways that are inconsistent with or contradictory to those earthly vocations. Yet, the way we Christians often tend to handle such truths can leave many singles feeling as if they have missed out on, or failed at, the purpose of being either male or female. As my never-married friend Michael has said, "The typical books which are pitched at

Christian men move very quickly into a narrative that says the end game for a Christian man is to be a godly husband and father". The same sentiment holds true for many Christian books pitched to women.

But here, too, eternity has something to teach us. In the new creation I will be my most perfect female self, while not being a wife or a mother. And so, from the perspective of the resurrection body, being a wife or a mother cannot be what defines or gives ultimate meaning to my femaleness. Yes, those two vocations are very good and meaningful expressions of femaleness in this creation. But, because they won't exist in and for eternity, they cannot be the definition of what it is to actually be a woman (or, correspondingly, a man).

So then, what is the definition or purpose of being a man or a woman? I promise we're about to have a go at answering all these outstanding questions! But let's first wrap things up here. Eternity teaches us that those who are not husbands, wives, fathers or mothers *have not failed* to live out their maleness or femaleness properly. Indeed, single Christians are living, breathing reminders that being a husband or a wife, a father or a mother, does not lie at the enduring core of what it is to be a man or a woman.

Men and Women Called to Love and Be Loved

Okay, so what then *actually* is the point of this whole sexuality thing God has given us?

Back in chapter 2, we saw that it was always God's intention to make humanity male and female, and that this had to do with them being made in his image (Genesis 1:27). As we read on in Scripture, we discover that, yes, married men and women were intended to have sex with each other, and this was a good and proper expression of their sexual natures. However, we also discover that men and women were intended to relate to each other, *as men and women*, and to do this in a myriad of ways that didn't simply involve marriage and having sex. God's word shows us that sexual intercourse is one (important) expression of human sexual nature in this creation, but that it is not the sum total of it.

From the very beginning, right through to the ever-after, God's purpose for male and female human beings has been to live and love as those who are the same (that is, we are all human) but who are also different (that is, we are not all males nor all females). This kind of loving relationship through sameness and difference is, in a very real and deep sense, part and parcel of our being made in God's image. He is of one essence but is three different "Persons". All of this means that God has given us our sexuality *so that we enjoy diverse relationships* through sameness and difference, not with just one other person but with many others. It's really as simple—but also as profound—as that.

I love how the theologian Stanley Grenz puts it: the "emotional and psychological dimensions of our sexuality [lie] behind the mystery of our need to reach out to others and [are] the basis of affection, compassion, tenderness and warmth".[30] When all is said and done, our sexuality (meaning, our sexual nature as males and females) exists so that we may love and be loved by those who are like us and those who are different to us. And this love will continue for eternity!

Looking in a Mirror Dimly Versus Seeing Face to Face
You might be wondering what it will actually be like for us to love and be loved by the opposite sex in a time when sexual desire and intercourse will be off the table. Or perhaps you are trying to work out why we will have sexually

differentiated resurrection bodies if we won't be using those bodies for intercourse and procreation. Will we retain our earthly sexual genitals? And if so, for what purpose?

These are interesting questions to ponder. Jesus' resurrection body was still very much recognisable as a human male body, and yet it wasn't exactly the same as his earthly body. He walked, talked and ate food—but he also did strange things such as moving through walls. The resurrected Jesus didn't just try defying gravity—he very much did defy it! And so, we might speculate that the physiological features of our resurrected bodies (including the sexed features) may not be exactly the same as our earthly ones.

But, "speculate" is the key word there. We simply don't know the detailed answers to these questions because God has chosen not to reveal them to us—at least not yet. The apostle Paul explains it this way: "For now we see only as a reflection as in a mirror; then we shall see face to face. Now I know in part; then I shall know fully, even as I am fully known" (1 Corinthians 13:12).

And so, as we grapple with questions about how our embodied sexuality now will remain genuinely meaningful in an eternity where there is no marriage or sex, we do so as those who are looking into a mirror and seeing only a dim, muddied reflection. We can make out the basic shape, but not the technicolour detail.

There is a day coming when not only will our questions be answered, but we'll actually experience the fullness of those answers in and through our own resurrected bodies. How amazing will that be! But that day is not yet here. For now, we are simply called to trust what God's word *has* made known about the future Christ has won for us, and to consider how that impacts our present. We'll explore some of those real-life implications next.

6

Let's Talk About Sex

Part 2: Living It Out

As eternity reaches into the present, it teaches us not just about sex itself but about what it means for us to be people who *are* sexual. So, let's explore what it might look like to live out some of these lessons. We'll mainly be zooming in on what they have to say to single Christians this side of eternity. But lest any married folks feel left out, I've got you covered at the end!

Being Single and Sexual

When it comes to sex and sexuality, those of us who are unmarried often hear little more than "No, don't do that", "No, that thing isn't for you" and "No, that's not for you to know". Because we are so used to being told that our sexual personhood is governed by one "No" after another, we can be left feeling isolated from and even at odds with our own sexual nature. As Susan said to me, "Living on a diet of No's has felt disheartening, dehumanising, prohibitive and, dare I say it, embittering". She continued, "It's like people view me as if I'm not a sexual being—like sexuality only belongs to people who are having sex. I feel invisible."

Many sexually abstinent never-married Christians can particularly feel infantilised, as if their being a virgin has left them trapped in some sort of perpetual Christian adolescence. Single-again Christians can also experience a sense of sexual "otherness" within their church communities. For example, Elizabeth and her husband were happily married for almost 23 years before he died. Now that she is a sexually chaste widow, she says people at church look at her "like some kind of alien!"

Yet, all of this doesn't simply leave countless unmarried Christians feeling disconnected from themselves or alienated from others. It can also leave them feeling disconnected from their Creator. For Jodie, "the thing I find hardest about being single is the lack of regular, heartfelt human touch. Physical closeness with others has such positive impacts on one's health. But so many churches don't acknowledge that this is a real struggle for single people. They rarely teach that healthy human physical connection goes beyond just having sex. It leaves me questioning why a good God would deny me, and so many others, this thing that is just so important in life."

A strict diet of sexual No's, turns the single Christian's sexuality into either a barrenness to bear, a reality to be suppressed, a tragedy to be endured or all of the above. But, as we have seen, Christ's eternity teaches us something different, something better, something far more life-giving.

Single friend, God has made you either male or female— that is, he has gifted you with a sexual nature. He wants you to embrace and express that in your embodied human existence. His vision and purpose for your sexuality isn't simply one "No" after another. Rather, he wants it to governed by "Yes" after "Yes" after "Yes". But, he wants those Yes's to be Jesus-honouring and other-person-loving.

Let's be real with each other. There is a fair chance that you have had, are having, or will have some sort of sexual activity outside of marriage. In his book *After the Revolution: Sex and the Single Evangelical*, David Ayers shows that 68% of unmarried American evangelical Christians who are between the ages of 18 and 22 and attend church weekly have engaged in either sexual intercourse or oral or anal sex. That number increases to 78% for those aged 23-32.[31] And with almost 65% of Christian men admitting they watch pornography once a month or more[32] (and those rates increasing among women too), there is a high likelihood that this may also be an area of sexual struggle and sin in your life.

God's word is clear. Our good Creator designed sexual intercourse (and all the other things that go along with it) for marriage. It's important for us to make sure we have that order right. Marriage doesn't exist to give us the opportunity to gratify our sexual desires. No, our sexual desires are purposed to serve God's purposes for marriage.

God gave us longings for sexual intercourse so that we might direct our eyes towards the earthly relationship in which those desires find their proper end—marriage. Then, within marriage and along with facilitating procreation, those desires are meant to foster and solidify the unique one-flesh relationship that a husband and wife share. And, as we have seen, this union is itself purposed to reflect the profound mystery of the union between Christ and his church (Ephesians 5:32).

In the end, our God-given desires for sexual intercourse are not really about us as individuals. Rather, they are designed to serve loving relationships with others and, ultimately, to lead us to anticipate the depth of intimacy to come between Christ and the church.

If you are unmarried and having sex (whether with your body or in your mind—see Matthew 5:28), you are turning your sexuality topsy-turvy in a very destructive way. You are rebelling against God by rejecting the purposes for which he gifted you with your sexual nature. On top of that, you are failing to honour the other person with whom you are having sex (with your body or in your mind) in the way God has designed you to. That person has not been placed in your life—or on this planet—so that they might gratify your sexual desires. Rather, you have been placed in their life to love them as the fellow image-bearer they are.

We must not be apathetic about sexual immorality. It brings hurt, harm and, ultimately, death. Jesus Christ was crucified so that you would be set free from your slavery to sin. In him, you are forgiven and have redemption. So friend, repent of your sexual sin and crucify the flesh with its passions and desires (Galatians 5:24). Do not allow your sin to enslave you to itself again.

Right now, you might be thinking, "She just said that my sexuality as a single person should be about 'Yes' after 'Yes'. But here she goes again with one 'No' after another." Friend, that complaint is the world speaking to and through you. It wants to convince you that the only thing your sexuality is good for is determining who you want to have sex with and the kind of sex you want to have with them. It wants to sell you on the idea that your sexual desires tell you who you really are. It wants to persuade you that unless you have the freedom to act upon those sexual desires, then your personhood is being suppressed.

But God's word tells you that when you say, "No" to misusing and abusing your sexuality, what you are *actually* doing is saying, "Yes!" to embracing and stewarding your sexuality. Your Creator didn't give you a sexual nature so that momentary orgasms could gratify you but so you could say, "Yes!" to living and loving as a sexually differentiated human being in this creation... *and* in the next.

And being single gives you particular opportunities to say, "Yes!" to embracing and expressing your sexuality here and now. When you faithfully say, "No" to sexual intercourse (or other related acts) as a single Christian, you are not suppressing yourself, nor are you being oppressed. What you are doing is saying, "Yes!" to wisely stewarding your sexual personhood in ways that are life-giving to yourself, loving to others and honouring to Jesus. So don't buy the world's lies. Instead, listen to and learn from God's truth. But also be willing to recognise that the world is very good at convincing us that we aren't listening to it when, actually, we are. Let me give you an example of what I mean.

I've noticed an increasing tendency among some single Christians to speak of their commitment to sexual abstinence as a kind of "sacrifice". Now, Romans 12:1-2 certainly encourages us to offer our whole selves as living sacrifices *to God*. But that's not the kind of sacrifice on view in these singleness discussions. Rather, an increasing number of single Christians now speak of their sexual abstinence as an unmarried person as a kind of sacrifice *of self*. As a personal cost which they nobly bear. Even as a kind of heroic martyrdom they are willing to endure because they think Jesus is worth the loss.

While godly obedience should be honoured, we must recognise that glorifying God and faithfully following Christ is *never* a sacrifice of our true self. It's actually us becoming the self that God created us to be, through the Spirit. Likewise, abstaining from sexual sin is never an act of heroism. Rather, it is an act of magnificent but also very ordinary Christian obedience. The single Christian who does not follow their fallen sexual desires is not a martyr among other Christians. They are simply (but also wonderfully) a faithful follower of Christ.

And so, thinking of chaste singleness as supreme self-sacrifice is the world masking itself in biblically-sounding affirmations. It is an outworking of the world's insistence that not acting on our sexual desires is nothing short of personal suppression.

God's eternity says differently. It says that the world has made far too much of sex itself and of our desires for it. Our sex drives are not the sum total or even the real essence of our sexuality. And so, there is much more to our sexual selves than merely our desire to have sex. Single Christians are in the excellent, even enviable, position of being able to take those lessons of eternity and help the church *really* learn them in the here and now.

Of course, knowing that truth doesn't erase the grief, pain, disconnection, frustration and isolation single Christians so often feel as sexually embodied creatures in *this* fallen creation.

It doesn't, for example, make our hunger for human touch magically disappear. For that, we need to retrain ourselves and others to understand that sexual purity doesn't require us to forgo all forms of culturally appropriate physical affection. After all, on five different occasions, 1st-century Christians were exhorted to greet one another with a kiss (Romans 16:16; 1 Corinthians 16:20; 2 Corinthians 13:12; 1 Thessalonians 5:26; 1 Peter 5:14), and Jesus commended the woman who expressed her deep love for him through the kissing of his feet (Luke 7:38-50).

Likewise, simply knowing the truth of our eternal privilege won't automatically change the way some in the church pity us as those who haven't experienced what is thought to be the best that life has to offer. In such situations, we need to remember it is Jesus Christ—not sex—that gives us life to the full (John 10:10). For this reason, we need to be willing to have humble, gentle, but frank conversations with each other (including our church leaders) when we notice that we're buying into the false promises of the "Sexular" world. We need to actively realign our vision for sexuality with God's vision and purposes for it.

Finally, knowing that we single Christians are forerunners of eternity won't make us suddenly immune to sexual temptation or sin. It won't mean that we are miraculously resistant to the lure of watching pornography, lying in bed at night lusting after that work colleague, indulging in same-sex-attracted fantasies, tantalising ourselves by reading erotic fiction, engaging in oral sex with the person we are (sort of) dating, paying someone to have sex with us, and so on. For that, we need the indwelling Spirit of God to do his sanctifying work in us. And yet, we also know we are not to sit back and just hope for the best. We'll spend more time considering what it looks like for singles to "flee sexual immorality [and] honour God with your bodies" (1 Corinthians 6:18, 20) in our final chapter.

But before we wrap up our discussion here, let me briefly address a practical question that may be on your mind—namely, how much sexual chemistry do I need to feel if I am to consider (or continue) dating, let alone marrying, someone? This is a complex question, not least because of some general psychological and clear physiological differences between men and women. But let me offer two principles that I hope may be helpful.

First, we shouldn't fall into the trap of making too little of sex in marriage. The one-flesh relationship is fundamental to God's purposes for it (1 Corinthians 7:1-3). This means that no marriage should be characterised by a complete absence of sexual intimacy (though, of course, there are seasons when this is heightened or lessened, and there may come a time when it ceases entirely). If you cannot begin to conceive of yourself ever having sex with someone you are dating, then I'd suggest you need to interrogate that inclination and discern how fixed or malleable it is.

And yet, this trap is not the one we are most vulnerable to today. Rather, we are far more likely to make too much of sex in marriage. Because we are prone to think that marriage was created so that we could gratify our sexual desires, we can be lured into thinking that full-blown sexual chemistry is a necessity from the outset. Yet, what we forget is that for thousands of years, human beings have married and had sex with spouses chosen for them by others, usually without any regard to the matter of their sexual chemistry.

Of course, experiencing sexual desire for your spouse is something to be welcomed and encouraged. But it is also something that can be kindled into existence.

Before becoming a Christian, my friend Rachel had enthusiastically embraced the same-sex sexual attraction she has experienced throughout her life. In her book, *Born Again This Way*, she describes how she had felt a sexual pull for past girlfriends "that seemed right out of songs and movies. It felt as unstoppable as a tidal wave."[33] Sometime after she gave her life to Jesus (and so repented of those desires and relationships), she met Andrew. Here is how she describes how the pull she felt towards him compared to what she had felt in the past:

Whereas the other feeling was overpowering and explosive, the feeling in me that was growing toward him felt much more vulnerable—like a small flame being protected by cupped hands from the wind.[34]

Rachel and Andrew gently kindled and nurtured that little flame and have now been married for well over a decade. Of course, their story is *their* story. And yet Rachel's words remind me of two truths. First, explosive sexual chemistry isn't always good or godly and shouldn't be the foundation for decisions about marriage (not the least because it can be misdirected and it often fades). Second, sexual attraction for a potential spouse can be kindled and built up as you deepen your knowledge, love, and service of them.

In the end, sexual chemistry is a part of our sexual personhood that is neither nothing nor everything. It is a creaturely reality that can either dominate destructively or be gently nurtured and carefully stewarded for God's purposes and in love of the other.

My single friend, we live in a world that too often insists sex is who we are. We might be part of a church that too often insists that sex is what we were made for. So, take lessons from eternity and show both the world and the church that, by making far too much of sex, we tragically make far too little of our God-given sexuality. By faithfully stewarding your sexuality in the present, you allow believers to glimpse the ever-after to come.

Being Married and Sexual

Finally, a word to husbands and wives. Both sex and child-rearing are very good and God-honouring ways for you to steward your sexuality in the present age. So, delight in them! Love each other better as a result of them. Use your bodies to serve one another. And remember that your sexual one-fleshness is meant to point you *and* the rest of us to the ultimate and enduring union to come between Christ and the church.

However, just because you may have this one part of the sex-ed lesson covered doesn't mean you get to skip the rest of the class. Here's the deal: your sexual nature is not simply about you being a lover to your husband or wife. It's also about being someone who loves your brothers and sisters in Christ, your family and friends, your neighbours and colleagues, even those who are merely acquaintances or strangers. To repeat the words of Stanley Grenz, your sexuality "lies behind the mystery of [your] need to reach out to others and is the basis of affection, compassion, tenderness and warmth". So don't short-change everyone else in your life by turning something that is about reaching out into something that only looks inward instead.

And please also remember that being a wife or husband (and potentially also a mother or father) does not define who you are as a male or a female person. Your sexuality— your sexual personhood—is fulfilled in more than those two good earthly outworkings of it. So don't find your ultimate identity in your sexual desires. But don't find it in your role as a spouse or a parent either. The perspective of eternity teaches us that as good as those things are, there is much more to who you are as a sexual being than just them alone.

Say No to This

Part 1: Burning with Passion?

By the time I was able to see a live performance of the musical *Hamilton*, I had already watched the original cast recording countless times. Being so familiar with the production meant that I noticed parts of the live performance I had missed while watching it on the screen. One of those came early in the second act when (#spoileralert) Hamilton is on the precipice of an adulterous affair. Watching live, I was absorbed in how the angst and turmoil of the moment was expressed on stage. I was particularly fixated on the ensemble swirling around Hamilton, heads in their hands, arms reaching out towards him as if to claw him back from the edge, repeatedly entreating him with cries of "No!" They were the physical embodiment of the song's title, "Say No to This".

When it comes to resisting sexual temptation, we Christians often think the idea of "Saying No to This" is little more than wishful thinking. Many of us resign ourselves to the idea that, without marriage, we are destined to an endless cycle of sexual temptation and sin. And the ensemble swirling around us—our church community, its leadership, other Christian influences—often agree that the only way to say no to sexual temptation is to say yes to marriage.

This was brought home to me during a conversation with a woman I'll call Sasha. She was in her late thirties, had never been married, and was struggling with sexual purity. "Dani, I have all these desires bubbling up in me," she said. "But I have no outlet for them. I don't know what to do with them." She recounted how, on a recent Sunday, the preacher at her church had said that if any singles in the congregation were struggling with sexual temptation, then they needed to heed the apostle Paul's words that "it is better to marry than to burn with passion" (1 Corinthians 7:9).

Even though he wasn't aware of Sasha's struggle, she said it felt as if this pastor was speaking right at her, telling her she needed to get married before her desires got the better of her. But what was she meant to do? She had been praying for marriage for years, all to no avail. She felt trapped, helpless and doomed. And she also felt angry at God. Why would he tell her she needed to get married to solve her problem with lust but then withhold marriage from her? How was she meant to indefinitely say no to sexual sin if she never had the opportunity to say yes to marriage?

In this chapter, I want to explore whether living a godly, sexually pure life truly is nothing more than an unrealistic pipe dream for the single (or single-again) Christian. I also want to ask whether marriage really is a ready-made solution for someone who struggles with sexual temptation.

Controlling the Burn

Let's start by taking a closer look at 1 Corinthians 7:9:

But if they cannot control themselves, they should marry,
for it is better to marry than to burn with passion.

The first thing to note is that in the original Greek the letter was written in, the word "passion" isn't there. Paul literally wrote, "It is better to marry than to burn". Period. However, most of our English translations add the two clarifying words "with passion" because that's the type of burning many scholars think that Paul probably had in mind. And there is good reason for that. The Greek word for "burn" *can* mean being aflame with strong (though not always sexual) passion.

However, the word can *also* refer to the metaphorical fires of God's judgment. Given that in this letter Paul had already spoken about the flames of God's judgment (3:15) and also specifically linked sexual immorality with that judgment (6:9-11), it's possible that he intended his readers to have that in mind as they read 7:9. Paul *could* be saying that it is better for someone to marry than it is for them to burn in judgment for their (sexual) sins. Or he could be saying that it is better for them to marry than to be aflame with (sexual) passion. So which is it?

In the end, I don't think we need to get too hung up on the answer to that question. Why? Because both lead to the same ultimate endpoint. In 6:9, Paul warns that "wrongdoers will not inherit the kingdom of God" (in other words, they will face judgment). And then, in the very next verse, he immediately goes on to specify that those who commit sexual immorality (that is, any form of sexual activity outside of heterosexual marriage) are included in the list of such wrongdoers. Burning with unrepentant sexual passion leads to burning in judgment.

But there *is* an aspect of Paul's burning comment in 1 Corinthians 7:9 that *should* catch our attention—

its all-consuming "ablazeness". The word translated as "burn" has an intensity about it. It is meant to bring to mind being consumed or, as the NRSV translates it, being "aflame". Paul doesn't have on view a simple arousal of sexual appetite. Rather, he is speaking about, and to, someone who is aflame with that appetite—ablaze with desire and consumed by it. He's speaking about someone who is actively entangled in sexual sin.

Here's the thing: in this epistle, Paul is not giving generalised ethical guidance to a massive faceless crowd. Instead, he's writing to a relatively small group of real people in Corinth (probably somewhere between 80 and 200 of them) who had been Christians for about five years at the most. Other parts of the letter make it clear that he knows these young Christians, the pressures they face, the questions they are asking—and the sin that is happening among them. And so, in verse 9, Paul is not raising a theoretical situation that may or may not be relevant. No. He is specifically addressing certain individuals, namely, unmarried Corinthian Christians who are actively committing sexual immorality.

We know this because, while our English Bibles usually translate this verse as something like "If they cannot control themselves..." (NIV), what Paul actually wrote is closer to "If they are not exercising self-control..." That is, the verb for exercising self-control is not written in a future, hypothetical tense ("if they cannot") but in the present ("if they are not"). So Paul is not saying that if an unmarried Christian doesn't think they are cut out for long-term singleness, they are under a moral responsibility to get married. Rather, he is actively calling out unmarried Christians who are *not currently* exercising self-control. He's speaking to single Christians who are entangled and ablaze with sexual sin.

Perhaps one or more of the unmarried Corinthian Christians was sleeping with prostitutes or slaves in their household (both of which were socially "normal" things for pagan men to do). However, verse 36 also suggests that sex may have been occurring between Christians who were betrothed to each other. In the end, we don't know the exact circumstances. But what we *do* know is that Paul says, *Cut it out! Remaining unmarried is good. But if you are out there having sex, then don't fool yourself into thinking that you are doing an honourable thing by remaining single. You know that the sexually immoral will not inherit the kingdom of God. And that is not who you now are. So, if you are choosing to have sex, then choose to get married. That's where it belongs. It is good to remain single. But it is better to marry than it is to burn.*

So this verse is not a general call to any unmarried Christian who experiences any sort of sexual desire to solve that pesky problem by getting hitched. No. In its context, the verse is saying that it's good to remain unmarried *unless* you are enjoying the "perks" of marriage without the actual being married part. It is better to choose marriage than to choose to remain tangled up in sexual sin.

Marriage Does Not Legitimate Lust

Now, this raises a whole bunch of questions about how Christian singles should rightly apply this verse today. We will turn to those questions in our final "Living It Out" discussion. But first, we need to talk a little more about marriage—because our usual (mis)understanding of verse 9 has some very significant implications for our thinking about that, too.

If we say that "ungifted" single people need to marry or, to quote Martin Luther, they are otherwise "bound to commit heinous [sexual] sins without end",[35] then we are saying that marriage is the remedy for heinous sexual sin. We are saying that a spouse is a solution for a person's lust (their "burning with passion"). Let me give you three reasons why I'm convinced that this kind of thinking about marriage is not just problematic but really rather tragic.

First, by suggesting (or even just implying) that marriage is a solution for lustful desires, we reveal just how deeply we've dived into the topsy-turviness of this fallen world. In Genesis 1 – 2 we see that God designed the one-flesh sexual union for marriage, not the other way around. And so, when we make marriage the remedy for our sexual desires, we turn that order on its head. We make them the fundamental reality, and marriage the thing which caters to them. But it's even worse than that: *we make our sinful compulsion to misuse and abuse the good gift of sex* the fundamental reality to which marriage caters.

Second, when we urge people to marry as a solution to their lust problem, we are in grave danger of encouraging them to see their spouse as an outlet for, or even a servant of, their sinful and selfish sexual desires. This stands in sharp contrast to how a passage like 1 Corinthians 7:3-5 talks about sex in marriage. There Paul writes:

> *The husband should fulfil his marital duty to his wife, and likewise the wife to her husband. The wife does not have authority over her own body but yields it to her husband. In the same way, the husband does not have authority over his own body but yields it to his wife. Do not deprive each other except perhaps by mutual consent and for a time.*

While the apostle's language may perhaps sound a little clinical to us, it is actually far from it (especially in a

1st-century culture that allowed women almost no bodily autonomy). Paul speaks here of a husband and wife mutually, willingly and lovingly giving their bodies over to serve the other within their marriage. This is the very opposite of lust!

You see, as the author Erik Varden explains, lust is not the same thing as simply experiencing any form of sexual desire. Rather, lust is different from "healthy desire" because it "is not directed towards communion, through surrender with another, but [is] intent on self-satisfaction, for which purpose another human being is instrumentalized [and] used as a means towards an end".[36]

Lust involves the idea of coveting. (Romans 7:7 and 13:9, for example, use the same Greek term for lust as the word for covet.) It's about using your eyes and your flesh to greedily grab hold of something that isn't yours *so that* you can use it for your own illicit purposes (Matthew 5:28; 1 John 2:16). Passionate lust is reckless and selfish, and belongs to the pagans, who do not know God (1 Thessalonians 4:5). Regardless of the context, lust is *always* an evil corruption of the sexual nature that God has graciously given us and a terrible abuse of the person whom we are lusting after. Marrying for lust is the very opposite of marrying for love. This is why Steve, a pastor friend of mine, says that a husband who lusts after his wife (or vice versa) commits an act of violence against her

Third and finally, in promoting marriage as the remedy for lust, we are setting people up for disappointment, hurt and even harm. Getting to have "legitimate" sex (in marriage) does not magically make lust disappear. A newly married couple do not wake up on the first day of their honeymoon suddenly cured of all their sinful sexual longings. No, they continue to struggle with their fallen sexual desires. Consider Jesus' words in the two passages below:

You have heard that it was said, "You shall not commit adultery." But I tell you that anyone who looks at a woman lustfully has already committed adultery with her in his heart. (Matthew 5:27-28)

But the things that come out of a person's mouth come from the heart, and these defile them. For out of the heart come evil thoughts—murder, adultery, sexual immorality, theft, false testimony, slander.

(Matthew 15:18-19)

Our Saviour makes it clear that we have a lust problem because we have a heart problem. Sexual immorality is the fruit of lust, and lust flows out of the sinful hearts of married and single people alike. Getting married won't rid our hearts and our minds of all the ways they desire us to misuse and abuse sex—and misuse and abuse our spouse in fulfilment of those desires. In fact, Satan uses whatever he can find in the circumstance we are in to tempt us away from the path of righteousness (e.g. 1 Corinthians 7:5). And so, getting married to solve lust is like taking a painkiller, not finding a cure. It will *never* solve the underlying condition because the only remedy for our sinful hearts is the redeeming gospel of Jesus Christ. We must not give to marriage (or singleness) what belongs to Jesus alone.

And yet, Paul's exhortation in 1 Corinthians 7:9 still stands: unmarried Christians who are engaging in sexual immorality should marry. If marriage isn't a cure for their lust, then why would he say that? Well, again, Paul is not making a blanket pronouncement about marriage being the way to control the burn (so to speak). Instead, he is simply saying that any unmarried Corinthian Christians who *are* choosing to sinfully covet and seize hold of a blessing of marriage—sex—ought to choose marriage itself instead. It won't remedy their lust. But if their decision is between carrying on in habitual sexual sin as an unmarried person or getting married and having sex within its God-ordained context, then their decision should be a no-brainer.

Being a sexual sinner is what some of the Corinthians were. "But," Paul tells them, "you were washed, you were sanctified, you were justified in the name of the Lord Jesus Christ and by the Spirit of our God" (6:11). And so, he says, *Be who you now are.*

The Remedy at Work in Us

If marriage won't solve an unmarried (or a married) person's lust problem, are we doomed to exist in an endless cycle of sin and shame? Are we forever unable to "Say No to This"? Not at all! One of the great blessings of the gospel is that it not only saves us but also sanctifies us. The remedy doesn't only work for us; it works in us.

Self-control is one of the wonderful ways in which the gospel transforms the lives of those whom Jesus has ransomed and rescued. We might be tempted to think of self-control as little more than a biblical footnote. But in reality, it is a major theme throughout Scripture. Indeed, the Bible considers self-control to be an essential characteristic of the life of discipleship (e.g. Proverbs 25:28; Galatians 5:23; 1 Timothy 2:9, 15; 3:2; 2 Timothy 1:7; 3:2-3; Titus 2:2, 6, 12; 1 Peter 4:7; 2 Peter 1:5-8 and others).

The world around us likes to depict ownership over our passions as being repressive or uptight—perhaps even frigid. But the Bible honours self-control as virtuous, even beautiful. Why is that? What is so good about self-control? To answer that, all we have to do is to consider the alternative. In 2 Timothy 3:2-5, we see a depiction of what it looks like to be a person who, among other things, is without self-control.

> People will be lovers of themselves, lovers of money, boastful, proud, abusive, disobedient to their parents, ungrateful, unholy, without love, unforgiving, slanderous, without self-control, brutal, not lovers of the good, treacherous, rash, conceited, lovers of pleasure rather than lovers of God—having a form of godliness but denying its power. Have nothing to do with such people.
>
> (2 Timothy 3:2-5)

Did you notice the emphasis on "love" in that passage? Those who lack self-control are also characterised as those who are lovers of themselves, of money and of pleasure. They are people who do not love the good and who certainly do not love God. And so, they are brutal, abusive, proud, treacherous and more.

The flip side is that self-control is a beautiful thing *because it is a loving thing*. As we exercise self-control over our bodies, we are exercising love: love for the God who created us to enjoy him for ever; love for others whom we are called to serve for their good (rather than use for our selfish purposes); even an appropriate love for ourselves as image-bearers of God and those whose bodies are the temple of the Holy Spirit (1 Corinthians 6:19).

And so, if you are a single Christian who struggles with sexual self-control, take heart! You don't require an extra special gift of the Spirit to be able to "Say No to This" because self-control is one of the (wonderfully!) "ordinary" fruits of the Spirit (Galatians 5:23). And if there are times when you do fail to exercise self-control as you should, then do not think of it as a one-strike-and-you're-out deal. It's not even a 101-strikes-and-you're-out deal. Earnestly repent before God, take refuge in Christ and reaffirm your commitment to cultivate this spiritual fruit day by day. Self-control is possible for you.

But self-control is also *good* for you... and for others. Yes, it is better to marry than to burn with passion. But what is even better than that is not burning in the first place! Prayerfully restraining your passions and bringing them under godly control is a beautiful thing. It is an expression of your love for your Saviour, your love for others, and even your love for yourself as one who now belongs to Christ.

Exercising self-control isn't easy. Often, it can feel as if we are the living embodiment of that *Hamilton* ensemble who swirl around in angst and turmoil. And yet, hard as it may be, self-control is good. It's the fruit we're called to cultivate as people who live on the threshold of eternity— an ever-after free from all temptation and sin. Self-control characterises the beautiful not-yet life we're called to live in the here and now.

Say No to This

Part 2: Living It Out

In the previous chapter we saw that, contrary to what we often hear, 1 Corinthians 7:9 is not a call for all unmarried Christians wrestling with any kind of sexual temptation to get married ASAP. Instead, this verse calls unmarried Christians who are not exercising self-control to take their sin seriously.

But how does this all apply today? How do we take Paul's words to a small group of new Christians in a 1st-century pagan city in ancient Greece and apply them to Christian singles immersed in today's hyper-sexualised, pornified Western world?

Same Same...

We might be tempted to think that Christians today are at "peak struggle" when it comes to avoiding sexual temptation. We're surrounded by sex on our billboards, in our songs, on our TVs, and in our social-media feeds. And then there is the evil lure of pornography, which is anonymously available 24/7. Those Corinthian Christians didn't have to deal with any of that!

But they *did* have to deal with prostitution that was not only legal but far, far more widespread and socially normalised than it is in our own time. They lived and worked in wealthy households whose rooms were covered in artwork that could only be described as pornographic. They were surrounded by literature and art that was sexually salacious. Women, adolescents and those who were slaves or of lower social standing were considered fair sexual game by the male elite. While Paul's original readers weren't dealing with the exact same kinds of external sexual temptation that we are, boy, did they have their own!

But even leaving those cultural factors aside, there is one inescapable thing that we definitely have in common with the Christians of the first centuries—our sinful human hearts. All of those sexualised elements of culture only exist because of that root problem. Whether it be socially accepted sex with a 1st-century prostitute or socially accepted sex with a 21st-century boyfriend, sexual sin can always find a way to be justified by our fallen hearts and minds. And so, Paul's ethical instructions about singleness, sex and marriage to the church in Corinth remain absolutely instructive for us today.

... But Also Different

Yet, we do need to acknowledge that there *are* some important differences between their time and ours. For instance, Paul speaks of getting married or remaining single as a fairly straightforward endeavour. And for many in 1st-century Corinth, it really would have been as simple as that. From a relatively young age, most of them would have been formally betrothed by their *paterfamilias* (the male head of their household). For better or worse, many of those whom Paul was writing to and about had a "ready-to-go" marriage partner. But the average 21st-century Western single Christian is in a decidedly different situation.

On one hand, many (though not all) single Christians today have far more personal decision-making power in determining who, when and why they marry. On the other hand, all of this personal agency sits on a finely balanced see-saw. Marital possibilities seem endless to the young unmarried Christian. However, the older you get, the narrower that horizon becomes. This is especially the case for single Christian women who, as they grow older, usually far outnumber their male counterparts (though some of the most recent statistics suggest the coming decades may see a complete reversal of this trend). Many unmarried Christian women and men would dearly love to be married. And yet, they can't just snap their fingers and make it happen. This means that they can be deeply pained by a (nearly always married) pastor insisting that they need to find themselves a spouse if they experience any sexual temptation at all. It can take everything in them not to stand up in the middle of the sermon and cry, "That's easy for you who got married at the age of 22 to say!" If that's you, keep reading, as we'll return to this soon.

But first, we do need to recognise that there are other single Christians who *are* burning with passion in the sense Paul means. These men and women can be tempted to hurry past this verse, or perhaps even ignore it altogether, precisely because it is so hard-hitting and uncomfortable. And so first, a word to them. Perhaps to you.

If You Are Single and Not Saying No to This

My dear brother or sister, if you are having sex outside of God's life-giving purposes for it, you are sinning against him. You are not loving the person (or people) you are having sex with as you should. And you are not living the life of freedom and fullness given to you in Christ. I know these are hard words to read from an author you don't know. But here are some more compelling words, from a far more compelling author:

> Flee from sexual immorality. All other sins a person commits are outside the body, but whoever sins sexually, sins against their own body. Do you not know that your bodies are temples of the Holy Spirit, who is in you, whom you have received from God? You are not your own; you were bought at a price. Therefore honour God with your bodies. (1 Corinthians 6:18-20)

If you are in a sexual relationship with a person you are not married to, you are not honouring God with your body. Indeed, you are sinning against your body. Please stop and repent. Flee from sexual immorality and delight in the assurance that "if we confess our sins, he is faithful and just and will forgive us our sins and purify us from all unrighteousness" (1 John 1:9).

But I also want to encourage you to do a second very confronting thing—namely, to give serious and prayerful consideration to the possibility of marrying that person you are having sex with. Now, let me be clear. There may be several *very* good reasons why that would not be a wise, spiritually mature or godly thing to do (including, but not limited to, them possibly not being a Christian). I am *not* saying that because you've had sex with someone, you must marry them. And, as I hope I've made abundantly clear by now, I am *not* suggesting that in marrying them, you'll find a remedy for your sexual sin. Furthermore, this should not be a decision you make in isolation from your loved ones, especially your church community and its leadership. Sin is masterful at confounding our discernment. Far too much is at stake for this to be something you work through alone.

And yet, even just considering the possibility of marrying that person will require you to reckon with the reality that you have chosen to enter into a one-flesh sexual relationship with someone that you aren't sure you could or should enter into a marriage relationship with. It will force you to confront the seriousness of taking what God designed to serve marriage and using it to serve your desires instead.

On the other hand, it may indeed be that you are free to and, all things considered, *could* marry that person. A friend of mine told me the story of two people at her church. The woman had grown up as a pastor's kid. The man was in the country on a student visa. They had sex and fell pregnant. The church leadership and congregation were committed to walking alongside this young man and woman in repentance, discernment, love and practical support. The two decided to marry. Now, years later, they both continue to walk with the Lord and each other; they have several children and are key leaders within their church community. This story is evidence of God's kindness in working for the good of those who love him, even in the very midst of sin. It also speaks to the vital importance of the family of God showing compassion, care and community to those who find themselves entangled in sexual sin.

My brother or sister, the Spirit longs to convict you of the folly of your sin and to inundate you with the joy of your forgiveness in Christ and the fullness of life that he has given you. And so, if Paul could have inserted *your name* at the beginning of 1 Corinthians 7:9, then please don't shut your ears to his word of rebuke and exhortation.

If You Are Single and Struggling to Say No to This

But what about if you are a single Christian who is not "burning with passion" in the specific sense Paul speaks about in verse 9 but who *is* struggling with sexual temptation in other ways? Perhaps you're in the throes of a pornography addiction or are absorbed by erotic fiction. Maybe you are wrestling with a sexual fixation on a particular individual or sexual attraction to people of your own sex. Or you might be someone who was sexually active in the past and worries about falling back into that sin in the present. What does this verse have to say to *you*?

Your singleness is good! However, its goodness does not excuse you from choosing or falling into sexual sin (more on that below). And so, if you have the choice to seek out marriage, then there can be great wisdom in doing that—provided you realise that it will not cure you of your lustful heart. And while we are on the topic, let me encourage you (again) to be on guard against any obsession with online (or offline) dating, viewing your church family primarily as a marital marketplace, or justifying marriage to someone who is not also a follower of Christ. Your godliness will not be served by an idolatry of marriage.

And yet, such idolatry is not the only threat to your godliness. Satan will be conspiring with your sinful heart and the "Sexular" world in which you live to lead you astray in other ways too.

He will be looking for opportunities to convince you that God is so disgusted by your deep-seated lust that there is no forgiveness for you. He would love you to feel so deeply ashamed that you can't even bring yourself to confess your impure thoughts to God. But don't give him that power. Remember, "God demonstrates his own love for us in this: *while we were still sinners*, Christ died for us" (Romans 5:8). Jesus knew exactly who he was saving and what he was saving you from when he set his love upon you. His grace is sufficient for you.

But Satan is *also* a master at minimising the seriousness of our sexual sin. So listen out for his whisper that it's okay to lust so long as nobody knows it is happening. Jesus says that looking at a person with lustful intent is the same as committing adultery with them in your heart (Matthew 5:28). And he considers this to be so serious that he immediately continues, "If your right eye causes you to stumble, gouge it out and throw it away. It is better for you to lose one part of your body than for your whole body to be thrown into hell" (v 29). God hates the sexual immorality that your eyes enable your heart to commit. He will judge it. So don't believe Satan's lie that it's no big deal.

Satan is particularly adept at persuading us not to make too much of any disordered sexual desires we might indulge our minds in. And on this, he has the world firmly in his corner. Both he and it want you to believe that desiring sex that is brutal or obsessively self-gratifying, voyeuristic or exploitative, with multiple people or with someone of your own sex, and so on, is no big deal—especially if you don't act on such desires.

But friend, sin has made your thinking futile and has darkened your foolish heart (Romans 1:21). This means that any desires of your heart and mind that are not aligned with God's order for your sexuality are caught up in sin's traction. They are not morally neutral. Moreover, our internal desires can so readily turn into external indulgences. As Romans 1 continues, "Therefore God gave them over in the sinful desires of their hearts to sexual impurity for the degrading of their bodies with one another ... to shameful lusts ... to a depraved mind, so that they do what ought not be done" (v 24, 26, 28). Sinful desires of the heart and mind rarely stay contained to just those parts of the body. So don't listen to Satan when he whispers that they are nothing to be too bothered about.

The gospel has freed you from guilt and shame over those disordered desires (more on that just below). Hallelujah! But that doesn't mean you should consider them any more neutral or insignificant than any other disordered desire, such as habitual gluttony or a propensity towards anger. We ought to lament that such instincts arise within us.

However, as you lament, keep in mind that Satan would also love you to think that you are enslaved to these desires and have no hope of ever being free of them. He wants to drive you to despair. But the Spirit whom God has given to his people "does not make us timid, but gives us power, love and self-discipline" (2 Timothy 1:7). Controlling your sexual desires is not an idealistic pipe dream but a fruit that the indwelling Holy Spirit is committed to cultivating in your life (Galatians 5:23). You have been spiritually empowered to exercise self-control! But take note of the verb there—exercise. Being self-controlled is not a passive activity. It takes focused, committed, *energetic*, Spirit-led, prayerful effort. It involves actively fleeing from sexual immorality (1 Corinthians 6:18)—running long, hard and fast in completely the opposite direction of it.

God's word exhorts us to "resist the devil, and he will flee from [us]. Come near to God and he will come near to [us]" (James 4:7-8). But what does it look like in practice to resist Satan, flee sexual immorality and draw near to God? Well, as we close, here are some suggestions.

1. CONFESS YOUR SINS TO GOD

Do this regularly—and particularly when you feel such shame over your sexual sin that you don't feel that you *can* face him. In that precise moment, draw near to God because "godly sorrow brings repentance that leads to salvation" (2 Corinthians 7:10). If you don't know how to begin your confession or what to say, then why not pray through Psalm 51:1-12? It is a beautiful, heartfelt template of confession and repentance.

2. DELIGHT IN THE FORGIVENESS & FREEDOM THAT IS YOURS IN CHRIST

It is right to lament your sin and disordered desires. But don't stop there. Instead, meditate upon the amazing grace that has put your sin as far from you as the east is from the west (Psalm 103:12). An example of that could be reading through a book like Philippians, which will help you reflect on "the surpassing worth of knowing Christ Jesus [our] Lord" (Philippians 3:8). Or perhaps cue up some of your favourite Christian music. I love listening to "It Is Well with My Soul":

My sin—O the bliss of this glorious thought!
My sin, not in part but the whole,
Is nailed to the cross and I bear it no more,
Praise the Lord, praise the Lord, O my soul.

3. PRAY DILIGENTLY

God's word promises that he "who began a good work in you will carry it onto completion until the day of Christ Jesus" (Philippians 1:6). He longs to make you more like his Son, so sit in a quiet room, lay your heart open before God and ask him to do that work in you. And if you are at a loss for the words to pray, then simply groan in the Spirit: "We do not know what we ought to pray for, but the Spirit himself intercedes for us through wordless groans" (Romans 8:26). God knows how to interpret those prayerful groans, and he knows how to answer them according to your needs and his will.

4. IMMERSE YOURSELF IN GOD'S WORD

The psalmist asks, "How can a young person stay on the path of purity? By living according to your word" (Psalm 119:9). Living according to God's word means you need to know his word. So, commit to a daily reading plan. Start a devotional series. Invite a friend to join you so you can keep each other accountable. Ask others what they have been learning from God's word and share what he has been teaching you. And, in those hidden moments when you most strongly feel the illicit tug of lust or disordered desire or pornography's allure, open your Bible and take immediate refuge in it. Stay on the path of purity by living according to the word of God.

5. GUARD YOUR HEART

The author of Proverbs advises us, "Above all else, guard your heart, for everything you do flows from it" (Proverbs 4:23). So, put into place wise boundaries designed to protect your heart from sin's allure. Make firm decisions about the kinds of movies and series you'll stream, the books you'll read, even the music you'll listen to. Set up accountability software for your devices. Consider what social-media apps you will and won't look at. Identify when your heart is most easily tempted (e.g. when you are tired, alone, bored?) and shore up your defences by going to bed early, calling a friend, or focusing on an enjoyable hobby. "Let your eyes look straight ahead ... Give careful thought to the paths for your feet and be steadfast in all your ways" (Proverbs 4:25-26).

6. DO NOT GO IT ALONE

We are to consider "how we may spur one another on towards love and good deeds, not giving up meeting together ... but encouraging one another—and all the more as you see the Day approaching" (Hebrews 10:24-25). So, commit to attending church every week, joining a Bible study or community group, attending prayer meetings or church retreats, meeting up with someone regularly to read the Bible and pray and so on. Moreover, pray for the courage to share the burden of your sexual temptation or sin with a mature Christian person (whether that be a friend or a church leader).

I know it can be absolutely terrifying to take that first step. But remember, that person has been given to you as your brother or sister in Christ. They are in this *with* you. So find them after church and have that initial conversation. Or pick up the phone during the week and make that first call. Here are some words you could try using: "I really need to talk to you about something I'm finding hard to deal with alone. Can we make a time over the next few days to have a private conversation? I need your help."

He Will Do It

That may look like a long list of things to *do*. But growth in this area is primarily something that we need God's Spirit to do in us. We need him to be with us, to strengthen us, and to transform the stubborn corners of our heart that are beyond our power to change. We will not make lasting progress in this unless we first admit that we cannot do this ourselves.

Paul establishes this in his first letter to the church at Thessalonica: "May God himself, the God of peace, sanctify you through and through. May your whole spirit, soul and body be kept blameless at the coming of our Lord Jesus Christ" (1 Thessalonians 5:23). Our sanctification is God's work. Our spirit, soul and body are *kept* by him. And here's the absolutely best part of it all: according to the very next verse, "The one who calls you is faithful, *and he will do it*" (v 24).

Conclusion

Time After Time

If I'm tired, stressed, or in need of a short break from everyday life, a lighthearted romantic novel tends to be my go-to. (That or an episode of the TV show *Taskmaster*—watch it and thank me later.)

It might sound odd, perhaps even a bit hypocritical, for the author of a book that extols the goodness of singleness to admit that she's a sucker for a rom-com! And yet I am. Why? Well, love—including romantic love—is a wonderful aspect of the human experience. And so it can be delightful to escape into such a story. But I've also found that the keyword there is "escape". I've honed my ability to enjoy a good romantic story without getting sucked into the vortex of wishing it was or thinking it could be *my story*. Like a reader of the fantasy genre, I enjoy it as something happening to fictional people in a fictional universe.

But there is another reason I'll often pick up a rom-com in those hectic or harried moments of life. It's because I know that a happily-ever-after is coming.

I find it comforting to read a story whose trajectory is familiar and whose ending is known. It allows me to enjoy the ride with a sense of non-anxious anticipation. I know things the characters themselves don't even know—namely, that all will be well that ends well. And so I read the story *through* the lens of the happily ever after I know lies on the horizon.

Friends, both the single and the married Christian life is to be read—indeed, it is to be lived—through the lens of the happily ever after that lies on the horizon. The life, death and resurrection of Christ has made the story's trajectory familiar to us. God's word has made the ending known. And so, we have the privilege of living life with confident anticipation rather than uncertain anxiety. We know that, in Christ, all *will* be well that ends well.

That end—a never-ending end!—is one in which there will be one loving husband, Christ himself, and one beloved wife, the church. How amazing is it that marriages on earth point us towards that ultimate reality. Together, as the body of Christ, we will collectively be joined in deep and abiding intimacy with our Saviour for all eternity. What an ending to live in light of here and now!

And yet that same never-ending end is one in which all of us, as individual members of the church, will not be married to each other. We will all be "single" ever after. Though none of us will be each other's husbands or wives, we'll have a depth of understanding and a loving togetherness that goes beyond anything we imagine. How amazing that singleness on earth points us towards *that* ultimate reality. What an ending to live in light of here and now!

Of course, knowing the end of the story doesn't mean we get to bypass all of the complications, messiness, pain, sadness or suffering that tragically is part and parcel of fallen life on this side of eternity. In his letter to the Romans, Paul writes that "the whole creation has been groaning as in the pains of childbirth right up to the present time. Not only so, but *we ourselves*, who have the firstfruits of the Spirit, groan inwardly" (Romans 8:22-23). This side of the ever after, we groan. But, as Paul continues, we also hope. Not for what is already present, for "Who hopes for what they already have? But if we hope for what we do not yet have, we wait for it patiently" (v 24-25). Living life now in light of the ever after to come—that is, what we do not yet have—means living with groaning patience but also buoyant hope.

Paul further confirms this for us in what I call his "resurrection manifesto" of 1 Corinthians 15. He begins by reminding the Corinthians Christians that Jesus "died for our sins according to the Scriptures, that he was buried, that he was raised on the third day according to the Scriptures" (v 3). He impresses upon his readers the absolute centrality of Christ's resurrection, for if "Christ has not been raised your faith is futile, you are still in your sins ... If only for this life we have hope in Christ, we are of all people most to be pitied" (v 17-18). But, he continues, Christ *has* been raised! And so, just as "in Adam all die, so in Christ all will be made alive" (v 22). And what an aliveness it will be! "For the trumpet will sound, the dead will be raised imperishable, and we will all be changed" (v 52). Mortality will be clothed with immorality, death will be swallowed up in victory, and the redeemed in Christ will all inhabit his happily ever after *with him*.

Unlike a rom-com, this love story is not fictional. Our immersion in it is not escapism. It is not a temporary reprieve from mundane reality. Rather, Jesus' love story *is* reality. And so, Paul closes 1 Corinthians 15 with these words: "Therefore, my dear brothers and sisters, stand firm. Let nothing move you. Always give yourself fully to the work of the Lord, because you know that your labour in the Lord is not in vain" (v 58).

Friend, our married *and* single ever after is coming. So whatever your situation in life, stand firm alongside your brothers and sisters in Christ. Let nothing move you or divide your devotion. Give yourself fully to the Lord and his concerns. And know that whether you have a spouse, do not have a spouse or no longer have a spouse, your labour in the Lord is not in vain.

We are all specialists in Christ's ever after. So, let's live now through the magnificent lens of the time that comes after time.

Chapter Titles Quiz

Did you notice that all the chapter titles in this book are song titles? For each one, can you name the artist? And the decade in which it was released? Once you've had a go, the answers are below!

Endnotes

1 Tyler Edwards, "Singleness Isn't a Problem," Relevant Magazine (March 24, 2023). https://relevantmagazine.com/life5/relationships/singleness-isnt-a-problem/.

2 J.P. De Gance, Nationwide Study on Faith and Relationships, Communio (2023), https://communio.org/study/.

3 As above, 13.

4 As above, 13-14.

5 As above, 14.

6 As above, 14.

7 As above, 15.

8 C. Peter Wagner, Your Spiritual Gifts Can Help Your Church Grow (Bloomington, Minnesota: Chosen Books, 2012), 54. Italics added.

9 Some biblical commentators suggest there is a good argument to be made that when Paul addresses "the unmarried and the widows" in 1 Corinthians 7:8, the word he uses for "unmarried" is better translated as "widowers". This would mean his comments here were intended to be directed specifically to those who are single-again after the death of their spouse (i.e., not all singles generally). While I think this argument has some merit, it's well beyond our purposes to explore it in detail. And so, for the sake of our own "unwrapping", we'll continue to follow most English translations in using the word "unmarried".

10 If you are interested in a deep dive on that, check out my exploration of the writings of some early church fathers here: Danielle Treweek, "Getting Historical About the Gift," (October 21, 2021). https://writing.danielletreweek.com/p/mythbusting-celibacy-2-lets-talk.

11 Stephanie Coontz, *Marriage, a History: From Obedience to Intimacy or How Love Conquered Marriage* (New York: Viking, 2005), 11.

12 For example, "in the new covenant intentional singleness is a "gift from God [...] instead of singleness being viewed as an anomaly, *intentional* singleness is now viewed as a gift given by God for service unto the Lord[...] *intentional* singleness is one example in the new covenant where the new creation has already begun to dawn". Stephen Wellum, "Singleness in the New Covenant," Christ Over All (29 May, 2023). https://christoverall.com/article/concise/singleness-in-the-new-covenant/. Italics added.

13 As above, footnote 1

14 Jerome Kodell, "The Celibacy Logion in Matthew 19:12." Biblical Theology Bulletin 8, no. 1 (1978): 19-23.

15 Danielle Treweek, "Return of the Eunuch (Part 1): An Enigmatic Passage," (December 12, 2024). https://writing.danielletreweek.com/p/return-of-the-eunuch-part-1-an-enigmatic

16 @PieterLValk, X.com, January 18, 2024, https://x.com/PieterLValk/status/1747669429469524286.

17 Pieter Valk, "Called, Not Conscripted (to Celibacy)," *Missio Alliance*, 23 March, 2023, https://www.missioalliance.org/called-not-conscripted-to-celibacy/.

18 Marshall Segal, "Single, Satisfied and Sent: Mission for the

Not-Yet-Married," *Desiring God* (13 March 2013). https://www.desiringgod.org/articles/single-satisfied-and-sent.

19 Lisa Arnold and Christina Campbell, "The High Price of Being Single in America," *The Atlantic* (January 14 2013). https://www.theatlantic.com/sexes/archive/2013/01/the-high-price-of-being-single-in-america/267043/.

20 Roy E. Ciampa and Brian S. Rosner, *The First Letter to the Corinthians*, ed. D.A. Carson, The Pillar New Testament Commentary (Grand Rapids, Michigan: Wm. B. Eerdmans Publishing Co., 2010), 6.

21 John Chrysostom, *Homilies on the Gospel of St. John and the Epistle to the Hebrews*, vol. XIV, ed. Philip Schaff, A Select Library of the Nicene and Post-Nicene Fathers of the Christian Church (Edinburgh: T&T Clark, 1877), Homily VII. https://ccel.org/ccel/schaff/npnf114.v.xi.html.

22 Augustine, *On Marriage and Concupiscence,* ed. Philip Schaff, vol. 5, Saint Augustin: Anti-Pelagian Writings, (Edinburgh: T&T Clark), Chapter 15.—The Teaching of the Apostle on This Subject. https://ccel.org/ccel/schaff/npnf105/npnf105.xvi.v.xv.html. Emphasis added.

23 Segal, "Single, Satisfied and Sent."

24 C.S. Lewis, *The Collected Letters of C.S. Lewis, Volume III: Narnia, Cambridge and Joy 1950-1963* (New York: HarperCollins, 2007), Letter To Mrs Johnson dated 8 November 1952

25 Stephen McAlpine, "A Sexular Age," (11 July 2015). https://stephenmcalpine.com/a-sexular-age/.

26 Martin Luther, *The Estate of Marriage* (1522) in *Luther's Works: The Christian in Society II*, ed Walther I. Brandt (Philadelphia: Muhlenberg Press, 1962), 18. Emphasis added.

27 As above, 18.

28 Martin Luther, "Commentary on 1 Corinthians 7," in *Luther's Works: Commentaries on 1 Corinthians 7, 1 Corinthians 15; Lectures on 1 Timothy,* ed. Hilton C. Oswald (Saint Louis: Concordia Publishing House, 1973), Vol. 28, Page 26.

29 John Calvin, *Commentary on the Epistles of Paul the Apostle to the Corinthians,* trans. John Pringle, vol.1 (Edinburgh: The Calvin Translation Society, 1848), 234.

30 Stanley James Grenz, *Sexual Ethics: An Evangelical Perspective* (Louisville, Kentucky: Westminster John Knox Press, 1990), 17.

31 David Ayers, *After the Revolution: Sex and the Single Evangelical* (Bellingham, Washington: Lexham Press, 2022), 131.

32 Joe Carter, "FactChecker: Do Christian Men Watch More Pornography?," The Gospel Coalition, June 8, 2020: https://www.thegospelcoalition.org/article/factchecker-do-christian-men-watch-more-pornography/

33 Rachel Gilson, *Born Again This Way* (The Good Book Company, 2020), 96.

34 As above, 96.

35 Martin Luther, "The Estate of Marriage," in *Luther's Works: The Christian in Society II*, ed. W. I. Brandt (Philadelphia: Muhlenberg Press, 1962), 21.

36 Erik Varden, *Chastity* (Bloomsbury Continuum, 2023), 77.

COMPANY

BIBLICAL | RELEVANT | ACCESSIBLE

At The Good Book Company we are dedicated to helping Christians and local churches grow. We believe that God's growth process always starts with hearing clearly what he has said to us through his timeless and flawless word—the Bible.

Ever since we opened our doors in 1991, we have been striving to produce resources that are biblical, relevant, and accessible. By God's grace, we have grown to become an international publisher, encouraging ordinary Christians of every age and stage and every background and denomination to live for Christ day by day and equipping churches to grow in their knowledge of God, their love for one another, and the effectiveness of their outreach.

Call one of our friendly team for a discussion of your needs or visit one of our local websites for more information on the resources and services we provide.

Your friends at The Good Book Company

thegoodbook.com | thegoodbook.co.uk
thegoodbook.com.au | thegoodbook.co.nz

About the Author

DR. RAE WYNN-GRANT is a wildlife ecologist who studies the impact of human activity on carnivore behavior and ecology. She received her BS in environmental studies from Emory University, her MS in environmental studies from Yale University, and her PhD in ecology and evolution from Columbia University. She is the cohost of *Mutual of Omaha's Wild Kingdom Protecting the Wild* on NBC and hosts the award-winning podcast *Going Wild with Dr. Rae Wynn-Grant*, produced by PBS. She is a National Geographic Explorer and has worked with National Geographic on a variety of televised nature programs, as well as a twenty-city speaking tour. Dr. Wynn-Grant has been featured in *Vogue*, *Forbes*, the *New York Times*, and the *Los Angeles Times*, among many others. She lives in California with her family.